DOOMSDAY'S DONUTS

DOOMSDAY'S DONUTS

Daniel Paul Jacobus

GSH

ISBN: 978-1-956074-42-0 (Paperback Edition)
ISBN: 978-1-956074-43-7 (Hardcover Edition)
ISBN: 978-1-956074-41-3 (E-book Edition)

Book Ordering Information

Phone Number: 315 288-7939 ext. 1000 or 347-901-4920
Email: info@globalsummithouse.com
Global Summit House
www.globalsummithouse.com

Printed in the United States of America

DOOMSDAY'S DONUTS ONE

Interior a television station like TBS. A woman interviewing an American Indian young man.

GUEST:
I was in a gated community when I read in the clouds, "Something
bad's gonna happen, something really, really bad.

HOST:
To erase the militant hypocracy of America's upper crust?

GUEST:
Everyone sees it but the inherent blindness is staggering.

HOST:
And your script retells the story of Revelations, correct?

GUEST:
Doomsday's Donuts actually.

HOST:
No one reads, knows about it, or really has the time—

GUEST:
To be plain it's about my vision. About the future. The Earth Changes. In order to get a reference point you have to go back--way back--to the cave man—the petroglyphs left by, who knows, the Neanderthal? Homo Erectus? The Hermits?

HOST:
Ha! Wonderful. Go on.

GUEST:
Two spirals: one goes counter clockwise, the one next to it, clockwise.
The young man holds up his palms waiting for rain.
HOST:
And it means evolution and devolution, right?

GUEST:
Not so fast, whirlpool eyes. One way one day, the other way the next. Pole shifts make the water drain differently.
The toilet flushes one way today and another way tomorrow.

HOST:
Help me out here. I

GUEST:
The earth turns one way and then.

HOST:
But the Mayan Calendar. The billions spent on the Super Collider.
The trillions lost due to the virus.

GUEST:
All hubris. A wet dream. We need food, shelter, underground, clean water and to be vetted by our Creator. This Mayan Calendar flap does not take into account paralax. Nine years off it is.

HOST:
And that is—

GUEST:
Paralax is the bending of light waves by gravity, which gives false readings. In 2012 the only thing that happened was

that earthquake and tsunami that ruined Japan. To this day they store tanks and tanks of radioactive water like a saki sogged swimmer waiting for the dam to break. And the white water rodeo.

HOST:
Everyone wants to know when the pattie will hit—

GUEST:
No one wants to be Moses after we're freed from our greed. But God has asked me to sit in. The Old Man's like a father to me. I'm trying.

HOST:
But what else do you have to say about the New Age, the New Age's dawn. Anything on your Hedge fund Buffalo Wallow?

GUEST:
When you see the Earth stand still, then five days later spin back the other way, you will want to have a copy of my musings at hand to determine what comes next. Either way I'm like gum on your boot, I'm not going away easily.

HOST:
And that's our scoop on the latest poop. This is PBS, until next time.

EXTERIOR: A SIDEWALK OUTSIDE STUDIO. A MOB OF GOTHS, SKATEBOARDERS, SURFERS, AND HIPPIES ACCOST KICKING ANTELOUPE THE CHEROKEE, THE GUEST OF FIRST SCENE.

MOB:

What about my IRA, man? Should we move to Nepal? This Ring of Fire really chaps my ass, Dude. Is suicide a sin? Does the Pope know this and keep quiet? Give me your child!
My temperature—

KICK:

People, people, listen: if I were to say all the nuns were my wives because I represent the bones of Christ, AND their domiciles belong to me. Then the nuns would know to feed me, take me to Clarksville. If I were to also say the Catholic Church is my property also, the birds must give in. If the Pope does not concede he will taste the blasted sock-it-to-me cake before his next birthday.

ENTER A HARI KRISHNA.

HARI:

What? Has Christ announced himself? Whoah. Take me with.

KICK:

No, now don't get me wrong.

ON EVERYBODY'S DEVICES, THAT INFERNAL SQUEAL. NEWS FLASH EMERGENCY.

CNN REPORTER:

We interrupt this program with a red hot news flash. A here-to-fore invisible meteor, a rogue rock, has just struck Italy. Mostly the Vatican. Your Vatican stamps are now priceless. But your prayers are, sorry to say, falling like fire from heaven. Yes, folks. A blindside by the cosmos has turned Italy's boot into a Payless fire sale slipper. More to come on the evening news.

KICKER TURNS ON A BULLHORN.

KICK:
All you nuns are hereby decreed squaws. Take off those weeds and put on summer dresses. Come out of two thousand years of mourning. Breathe the astral light.

MOB:
Vatican fathead! Pope immobiler! Kill! Kill! Kill!

KICKER DISAPPEARS IN A CLOUD OF SMOKE AND FIRECRACKERS.

MAN:
I saw that!

MAN STRANGLES FELLOW RIOTER.

SURFER:
You can't fool me, Jesus. I'll beat you back to your crib.

SURFER BEATS MAN STRANGLER.

MAN:
I'm seeing stars, Mr. Casey. Stop the predictions already.

SURFER:
Ah, so now you're a horoscope writer. Astrology is paganism. And Paganism is atheism. Atheism is Godless as science. Kill all the scientists and their astrologers. Bring out the snakes, scriptures, and beds

of coals to writhe and cuddle on. Faith!

WOMAN:
Quit breathing nonsense--my head is swimming with your bacon breath already, Freddy.

SURFER:
This ain't an Olympic trials, honey. You turned the wrong way at the last YMCA.
WOMAN:
Everything is wondrous. God would never decimate his sheep herd and give Fenris a toothy target. Would he?

PREACHER WITH A UKULELE.

PREACHER:
Man's power will be clarified when he turns into fertilizer. Fire to clean, waves to wash, mud to clothe, and crop the dust of Pompeii.

SURFER:
If I only knew the day I'd short the index.

PREACHER:
What disaster are we dismissing as we streak across the cosmic void?

END SCENE.

SCENE OPENS. THE RESERVATION. AT A SWEAT LODGE.
KICKER AND MEDICINE MAN.

KICKER:
I want to see God.

MED:
Okay, the exuberance of youth. You fast and sweat?

KICK:
Yeah.

MED:
Now you take these buttons from the Great Spirit's navel. Wash it down with orange juice as a catalyst.

KICK:
Yucko.

MED:
Go on now. You can only swallow as much as you can handle.

KICK:
Turn into a sparrow and feather tomorrow.

MED:
You'll really sing in half hour or so, warbler.

KICK:
Hum. Yuck. Hum. Hey, tastes like Miranda. Miranda's butt..

MED:
Now we're really fishing, shovelhead.

KICK:
I hear the train. Horses.

MED:
Whah—

KICK:
The angel. Gotta take this call.

HE GOES INTO A TRANCE. A VOICE SPEAKS. COYOTE APPEARS TO ADVISE KICKING ANTELOUPE.

VOICE:
There's gonna be a war. A war. A war. Enslaved scientists will create a venereal disease that crazes women into nymphos and turns men into rutting dogs. The seasons slide. Islands fall, mountains rise. Neo-nazism flourishes. Raise the flag, rah rah rah. Go, Betsy. The Ring of Fire erupts. The overpopulated and insane planet will find release in a blaze. Immediately over half of mankind expires. The wobbling of the earth gets worse. The poles shift. The spinning of the globe stops. In a flash most cities are flattened. Welcome the start of tribes and clans. Women rule politics and take back the primal sage brush. Chaos ensues as the dead cry out for company. Money's worthless. Only food and brutality have currency. A mini ice age comes along. The seas freeze. A new age follows, of more temperate climate. So go. Get up. Unite the tribes and save The People.

KICK:

Wow. Did that just happen or what? Damn.

MED:
So the Great Spirit spoke to your soul.

KICK:
Oh yes.

MED:
Well, watch out what you wish for when you say—

KICK:
I want to see God.

END SCENE.

A STREET IN ANYTOWN, USA. A MOB. TIRES AFIRE AND CARS TRASHED.

COP:
Monopoly made millions teaching capitalism to kids; but now we know how market days blow away all the pigs.

HOBO:
My food stamp boss lady so hateful and thinks me ungrateful. We pay her wages, pet her pet red tape worm, to vet hog troughs unabated.

STREET PERFORMER SALLIES ALONG WITH UKULELE.

STREET:
One strain for the monkeys one for the junkies, one strain for Midland one for Highland Park, one strand for Netherlands another for the better lads, colder in Mule Shoe than it is in Alaska.
One Ring of Fire to blast the way forward and a dust cloudy to shroud the morbid smores. Jet planes to spread'em and hypos to dead'em. One olive two pits, announcing the nut snip.
Oh drip away, trip away, slip away fortune. Join me in my mad refrain, we have gamma rays of the brain.
All will rue the day when Rue de Maine crumbles.

STREET PERFORMER MOVES ON AT COP'S BIDDING. JUGGLER ENTERS.

JUG:
Domino the pit bull licked his monthly statement.

On he spewed a funky brew avatar of a hot cave in. Cover your ears. Think nothing queer. It's just an animalistic digit. Stumbling over blue weavos and barfing at Gidget.

JUGGLER MOVES ON.

COP:
Fools! This Judgment Day snafu is merely froth, air, a bubble. We're on our way to making these bodies incorruptible. Right, Alexa?

HOOKER WALKS UP.

HOOKER:
Yup. Senior's on top, Junior's in the middle, and Trey is on the way to a new membership; that is after the aftermath's numbers crash to zero. Plus tax and depreciation, Officer. Pig and pooky never go out of style.

END SCENE.

EXTERIOR: A MESA IN THE DESERT. MEDICINE MAN AND KICKER ON CLIFF LOOKING AT VISTA.

KICK:
What are we lookin' for? What a climb!

HE SITS ON A ROCK.

MED:
Have you got your gun handy?

KICK:
What? What is it? A dying moose? An elephant? Tell me.

MED:
You see that dark cloud hugging Slash Mountain?

KICK:
The one that looks lonely?

MED:
More like a buffalo wallow, my boy.

KICK:
What does that mean?

MED:
The buffalo is bathing in a cloud of dust. He cannot see the brave crawling up to whap his horn with a coup stick. Then invite him to his teepee.

KICK:
So it's the end of the buffalo bath for Bubbles.
Right.

MED:
Now's a good time to bet against green grass and summer rains. How much cash do you got?

KICK:
All I got is the 300 tax return dollars. I was going to patch the roof of the trailer.

MED:
A great grub steak. The start of a promising fortune. Go bet the stock market will stumble a little this week. Well?

KICK:
I was just getting acclimated. My blood is thickening.

MED:
Do the mating dance on the way down.

KICK:
I'm gone. Wish me—

MED:
Your parents wished you into a crib. But good luck, Kicking Anteloupe.

KICK:
Thanks.

MED:
De nada. It's a—

KICK:
Long climb down, from the clouds. Long climb down, from the clouds. Long, long, long climb down. We'll take advantage of the leverage. Mommmmmaaaaaaah!

KICKING ANTELOUPE STUMBLES DOWN THE CLIFF.

END SCENE.

EXTERIOR: WALL STREET SIDEWALK. A MAN WITH A TELESCOPE ON A STAND.

TELEMAN:
I search the galaxies for a supernova to warm the dashboard of my stupid Rover. Spiral solar systems and giant black holes blow my mind and tweak the poles. If I can catch a comet sliding past Earth I zoom along as it smokes our turf. Mighty meteors make for ironic rain as the acne of Luna pops and strains. Clouds of cosmic dust dissolve and gather as the universe decrees planetary character. Seen the light and dark matter, astronauts, as gravity waves blast, scream, and rock the rafters.

TELEMAN STAKES OUT ANOTHER PATCH. KICKER BEING HOUNDED BY A NEWS REPORTER HOLDING MICROPHONE.

NEWS:
Where do you get your stock tips?

KICK:
Where does Aurora sleep? Where do thoughts come from?

END SCENE.

INTERIOR: THE WHITE HOUSE. THE PRESIDENT AND FIRST LADY WELCOMING VISITORS TO DINNER.

PREZ:
Welcome. Welcome. Looking good.

FIRST LADY:
Sheep and simians.

KICKING ANTELOUPE ENTERS.

KICK:
Kicking Anteloupe of Buffalo Hedge Funds.

PREZ:
Yo, Kicker. Glad you could come. Have some shrimp.

FIRST LADY:
We'll keep a hot wash cloth handy. Enjoy.
Eat. Be hairy. Watch out for the wiggling appetizers.
They'll chew you to pieces. Really, darling.

KICK:
Great advice. I got my taser.

VIXEN APPROACHES.

VIXEN:
Heya, Crazy Horse. Would you cry if I took you over
Niagra Falls holding onto your medicine ball?

KICK:
Uh. No.

VIXEN:
You must be hiding your kayak for emergencies.
Wanna go canoeing? I got a can of bait waiting.

KICK:
We'll see. First I wanna pow-wow with Thunder, run
with Lightning, and swim the dessert for scorpions.

VIXEN:
I hope you brought a long spoon cause some of these
gravy boats are yumscious.

KICK:
I never leave my tent without it. It's like my nose.

VIXEN:
Quit! That tickles. Ah, sharp and randy, I love it.
Let me do the honors. That's Melinda Gates, looking
for a hole to hide gold in. This man's Joe Biden.
Don't get too close, he's got creepy tentacles. Here's the
Guru of Omaha selling insurance and coal. Don't ask
for a quote, he just woke up after rereading his stock
portfolio. To half the room.

KICK:
Yeah, but where's the excitement? The split trousers?
The sterno breathing dragons?

VIXEN:
Come on, let's go powder our snozzes and smell
the roses.

KICK:
Well, rosin my bow. I thought I'd gumbo and hit the bullseye, then snooze atop a tub of ice cream.

VIXEN:
No, not this trip. We'll climb the foothills, then jostle the Rockies.

KICK:
I forgot my boots. Fiddle sticks.

END SCENE.

INTERIOR: HOTEL ROOM. KICKER AND VIXEN IN BED.

KICK:
So now that we got that over with, you can serve me with the paternity papers.

VIXEN:
I'm an anonymous senator's daughter, disinherited with a weak will and strong odor.

KICK:
I thought it was my horse sweat coming back to flog me.

VIXEN:
It is you that I have wanted. You get me. You're like manna from heaven topped with clover honey.

KICK:
Hold that thought, room service.

KICKER PICKS UP PHONE.

VIXEN:
Eggs 'n' toast. Coffee. I'm the most important meal of the day, Skeeter. But first a shower. Last one in gets a damp towel. Stale air. A froggy mirror.
Gummy razor. The afterbirth.

KICK:
You strumpet. Dog! After that I need something for the road.

VIXEN:
Oh, okay. Plenty more where that came from I'm sure.

HANGING UP PHONE, HE JUMPS UP OFF BED TO FOLLOW VIXEN.

END SCENE.

EXTERIOR: IN FRONT OF STOCK EXCHANGE, KICKING ANTELOUPE TALKING TO MOB OF INVESTORS.

KICK:
We have nothing, zip.

MAN:
Zero to a trillion and back in five seconds.

KICK:
Nothing to hide. If the England is underwater, look to it. If the mark is strong, ditto. If an auto company practices fraud, there's found money.
When an airline or plane builder's hiding a whopper, lunch is served. Look no further. If you're only half sure hedge the azaleas. Simple as sunrise.
But what will you do if the sun forgets to rise?
Huh!?

WOMAN:
Oh hell. Mysticism. I hate getting up for popcorn.

KICK:
Think! I'm not your dog to whip and punt.

KICKER EXITS THROUGH MOB.

GIRL:
Kicker! We still believe in greed.

NEWS REPORTER IN BACK GROUND.

NEWS:
The Buffalo Hedge Fund is only a nickel ahead as of today. What the roadblock is no one knows. Some pundit said his wife is sick. Best wishes to Buffalo Maiden.

END SCENE.

EXTERIOR: ATOP THE MESA. A FUNERAL PYRE.
KICKING ANTELOUPE TOSSES A TORCH. THE CORPSE AND WOODPILE
INCINERATE. DRUMS. CHANTING. KICKING ANTELOUPE
PICKS UP A BOWLING BALL BAG AND TURNS AWAY FROM FIRE.

KICK:
I am alone. But I will keep your head in liquid nitrogen just in case the future holds a benign wizard. Your revival to behold. And the perp.
Astounding! How many houses do you need? So many spouses drain your seed. How many greenbacks do you burn? So few cavemen to rule the world.
How many folks do you ride down when the headless horseman howls? How many hot dogs can you eat when Fido heats your meat? How many shit storms and your slime absolve your wad of doing time?
How many trumps are in Little Casino? Grab the cunts and fool the people. How many bumps 'neath your gator burning cross the mob of haters?

END SCENE.

EXTERIOR: CLIFF HIDEAWAY ABOVE DESERT. KICKING ANTELOUPE AND MEDICINE MAN SITTING, CHEWING
GRASS.

KICK:
That wasn't supposed to happen.

MED:
I'm dead too. Idiot.

KICK:
You never said—

MED:
Nothing's a pretty empty message to send to those who are EMPTY HEADED!!

KICK:
I'll try harder.

MED:
That's what the thunder bird told the raven, after he smashed all her eggs, her nest, cousins, and the mountain top with ten bolts of lightning.
You've hooked a monster of the deep. Strap yourself in. Hitch your tail bone to the magma's core.

KICK:
Got it. But what if I miss?

MED:
What does a ghost say to a grizzly? Boo!
Look in the sky! See?

KICKING ANTELOUPE STANDS UP, JOGS IN PLACE.

KICK:
All I see is chaos. And one lone buffalo calf sobbing.

END SCENE.

EXTERIOR: AT A STOP LIGHT COPS PULLING OVER A BLACK DRIVER.

COP:
Git out the cah.

BLACK:
What I do this time? Huh, man. Is it cause I'm a tar baby, Baby? Say it. You black.

COP:
Git out now. Now.

BLACK:
You don't got the balls of a pigskin quarterback!

COP:
If you insist.

COP SHOOTS BLACK GUY IN DRIVER'S SEAT. THEN HE EMPTIES HIS REVOLVER.

BLACK:
Oh, moma. Goodbye. Killer! Burn the last page, Trumpet Cherub.

END SCENE.

INTERIOR: A LIBRARY IN A HOME. DETECTIVE WITH TWO GUNS SITTING AT DESK.

MAGNUM:
Got fed up devouring perps so I decided to eat my gun.
If you think it's cynical you're not the only one.
Forty-five, forty-five, clean my whiskers and tan my hide. Forty-five
or .357, which tunnel burps wormholes to dreamy heather?
If you're cleaning up my brains, hon, 'tis the season to move on. Hate! Adrenalin! make me rage, bury my body then turn the page. Move over, dad; a lil' space, ma; don't neber say, It's against the Law.
Forty-five or .357, which shooter seeds the heather?

END SCENE.

INTERIOR: THE SCIENCE INSTITUTE. SCIENTISTS AND SENATOR FRANK.

SEN:
Let me understand this correctly—

SCI ONE:
We don't know why. Sometimes the dawn is early, sometimes she's late.

SCI TWO:
The Mother Earth is pregnant.

SEN:
Hogwarsh. Did the meteor do it?

SCI ONE:
Asteroid.

SEN:
Asteroid--hemmoroid--anal flux! Horse shit!
I wanna know!

SCI TWO:
But we ourselves don't even know. It's out of our purview.

SEN:
You'll be out of the sight of funding too
if you don't answer truly. It's the wobble.
It's creating a vortex. And from this
vortex wormholes to and fro past pole-shifts.
Don't double talk when I expect--answer.

SCI ONE & TWO:
We don't know nuthin'.

SEN:
Ah, finally. Pack up your Superman lunchboxes. You're cut off from free chocolate milk indefinitely. I'm chopping the vine.

SCI ONE:
Vine? we're not growing any vine at all.

SEN:
You're headed to the vinter and about to be squashed flat, green ovo. See you in the barrel.

SCI ONE & TWO:
Barrel??!

SEN:
The barrel of monkeys looking for a job, Chardonay. Lookin' for a yob.

END SCENE.

EXTERIOR: WALL STREET OUTSIDE THE STOCK EXCHANGE. KICKER AND MOB WITH COPS ATTENDING THE CROWD.

KICK:
The market has rebounded. Well. Let's put
our money on a downturn soon. Burger joints,
retail, auto parts, pawn shops, convenience sto's.
Walmart, Walgreen's.

TRADERS:
Gotcha, Boss.

EXIT BROKERS TO BUY AND WHEEL 'N' DEAL.

KICK:
Chaos, do your magic, girl.

POLICE CAR WITH BULLHORN BLARING.

COP:
Curfew is nine o'clock. I repeat, nine o'clock
curfew. Attention. Listen up. Off the streets—

KICK:
I know what that means: bang, bang owzie county.

RIOT OVERWHELMS POLICE PRESENCE.

VOICES IN MOB:
There goes my holiday. Time to feed the baracuda. Hoodoo you love; voodoo this suckah. Don't crack my smile or I'll slap your cheek to the Southside mile. Thank you, Lord, for

relieving yourself in my cup of wormwood tea. Sweet. Now I know what formaldehyde tastes like in my face. Hereafter I'll watch out for Legionnaire slime too. Gang, let's go make compost.
On to Mold Row and Bacteria Ballroom. Bring me to the Pecos, lower me amongst the cottonmouth, trade my temples for elephant ears, bless me, muddy pontiff. Lay me down in a spongy bed, water snakes and gar to be fed. Wash my sins away with cattails, a holy boat and rotten sails.
Make a pyre of my raven wings, pray for heaven as we sing.
Join the perch in a shad parade as we watch our bright sun fade.
The hour comes, the seconds gallop, the turnip yells dirt at the carrot.
Who will say raddish at my grave, drop the clods on my garish face?

KICKER'S TWINS ENTER.

GEL:
Dad?

GEL & BOY:
We're hungry.

KICK:
Ay, it never ends.

BOY:
Are you out of funds, Hedgeman? Impossible!

GEL:
I got a nickel for your financial pickle, warthog.

BOY:
Get us to the store on time. I will help you do your mime.

BOY GESTURES: MONEY!

KICK:
March, soldiers.

GEL & BOY:
Pow! Pow! Pow! Pow! You're dead! No, you!

END SCENE.

EXTERIOR: THE ROSE GARDEN. THE PRESIDENT HOLDING PRESS CONFERENCE. BLATHERING.

PREZ:
I am sending out the National Guard. They're getting fat and sassy and long for April, er March.
Flowers.

NEWSGIRL:
Are you initiating martial law? Truth.

PREZ:
I am giving a speech here, Darlin'.

NEWSGIRL:
I am not your darlin', horndodg.

PREZ:
Don't get snippy or you'll get gimpy.

NEWSGIRL:
Are you threatening me, Big Boy?

PREZ:
Freedom of speech. Freedom of speech, judge.
As I was saying before I was. . .

NEWSGIRL:
Well, bring it on, you up-jumped slum lord-ling.

PREZ:
Would you please put your boxers back on and leave? Security!

NEWSGIRL:
You can't toss this arugula before you Eat me!
Gargantua cyclops. Frankly I bought this seat with my Senator
Farther's vote. So there!

PREZ:
The embarrassment I have to endure—

NEWSGIRL:
To wave your snitzel. Yeah, yeah, we know each vein and wrinkle.
Man! Get your scrotum off my nose wart, tangello-pants.
Get on with it, Jack Horner.
The ice caps are melting. My contraception is about to expire.
Keep that missile down. You'll need it later for your adenoids:
to cauterize the bleeding where I have placed my flag, my red
flags, Brama.

PREZ:
What is goin' on here?

NEWSGIRL:
The two party system, Benedict.

PREZ:
I'm not bent.

NEWSGIRL:
You are too. I got photos to prove it. Here's you with your hand
in Puto's pants. Last New Year's.

PREZ:
I need a recess, America. She and I need to get one thing straight
between us.

NEWSGIRL:
I heard that. Let's go, you orangutan dance troop leader. I'll make you sing like the Mormon choir.

END SCENE.

EXTERIOR: ATOP THE MESA BESIDE A CLIFF, MEDICINE
MAN AND KICKING ANTELOUPE.

KICK:
What's the secret of life, Rolling Thunder?

MED:
The secret's out! We have to find out at Butler Shoes what it is that moves us. Life is our cake walk.

KICK:
You say that like—

MED:
Soon, too soon, sad to say, I'll disappear.
Sage smoke, windy day.

KICK:
So it will just come down to me.

MED:
It's like sex. It just comes. Just keep on humpin'.

KICK:
I want so much. But have so little. My bones ache already.

MED:
You have your third eye. Follow your dreams.

KICK:
I see too much. Nightmares.

MED:
Sleep with a pair of shades. Horse blinders,
Winky. Or nipples.

KICK:
That's as absurd as loving the woman of your dreams.

MED:
Absurdity is certainty in a country with glass curtains. If wisdom could be transmitted in a book, a picture, sculpture, we would all be all-powerful after detention ends. But the man of action acquires all the wine, women, and smarts. So it's a contradiction.
Mucho thinking--skunked!

KICK:
If I tried to leave my knowledge and wisdom to my kids—

MED:
They'd piss in your Life cereal anyway. And call you a dumb ass clown unfit to keep around as a bald broom in a shag den.

KICK:
Ignorance, the last refuge of progressive youth, and the hope of Tamara.

MED:
You're finally getting it, Campo. I can die in peace. Thank you, Raven and Coyote Trickster.

END SCENE.

EXTERIOR: LOS ANGELES AT NIGHT. A COMET STREAKS THORUGH THE SKY. A MAN WITH GUITAR ON SIDEWALK.

GUIT:
These are the days of hate and darkness.
It bodes thick roads of LaLa Parking
Pack it up, gas up the Winnebago.
Don't forget the hammock and the bagels.
La la la la la la parking. Shoot the haters
And stray aardvarkers. La La La La—

ANOTHER METEOR SHOOTS ACROSS THE DARK SKY GOING THE OPPOSITE DIRECTION NARROWLY MISSING COMET.

GUIT:
Where will you go when Aster comes crashing your party? How will you react when Sue Knobby is gravy? What cave will you cork when Sonnie misbehaves? Whose cheek will you grasp when the Finger of Fate offers a knuckle sandwich? Where will you hide when Morfiend comes calling your name? Shouting: "Don't try to shine me on!" Worm, squirm; wiggle and burrow.

ENTER BUM WITH WIFE AND KIDS.

BUM:
Do you have a light? Do you have a square?

KID:
I lost my GI Joe by the creek.

GUIT:
Gas it up, pack the Winnebago.
Paint your shoes with a bit of dayglo.
Shoo the bedbugs and glug some Dago red.
La la la la la la la parking. . .

RADIO SOUNDS.

RADIO:
The forecast is continued darkness until—

GIRL:
Look, lights in the sky. UFO's. UFO's.

WOMAN:
Where they come from no one knows.
Beta Retulae, the belt of Orion;
In the evening, in the morning.

KID:
They zoom into our lives, twist our fishing lines.
Visit oil free submariners; Hello! Hello!
Nuclear warning. Waiting for to vault,
Ezekiel's vision; the shadow effect of television.
They crease our wheat field crops,
Flash our sheets and socks. Suck up to our lakes;
Abduct our grans and flakes. Leave us our
bad dreams for goodness sakes. Buzzing jet
fighters, implanting SARS and daughter. Setting
an example and dropping off apples.

GIRL & KID:
UFO's: why they watch us no one knows.

MAN:
If a UFO shines his light on me, I'm going
to go to that shore by Galilee.

WOMAN:
Good luck, buster. Breeding cattle and
gutting steer.

KID:
I'm not a cattle, I'm a dogface soldier.

GIRL:
I'm hard to drive or park and so no steer.

KID:
Come on, Sis. Let's go find a burger joint.

GIRL:
Or a joint laced with comet dust.

EXIT TWO SIBLINGS. MAN FACES GUITAR PLAYER.

MAN:
You see what your music has done: it's
split up my family.

GUIT:
Life is hard for the star-crossed
pedestrian beside LaLaLaLaLa Parking.

EXIT MAN AND WIFE.

GUIT:
There's a riffle in the baffle that blows

the astral wind forwards and backwards.
A rent in the veil that conjures our spell.
A tear in the tapestry of our reality's happening.
A poke in the eye of our cyclops fantasy.
Whatever it is our vortex starts to spin
As the moving of artic poles unhinges our shoals.
Our souls feel the grind of the Cosmic Mind.
A storm in space makes our hearts begin to race.
There's a changing of the seasons without time or meaning.
When it falls and soars, Fenris wolf at the door.
As we try to pick up the pacing of the Fate we're facing.
It's time to separate the man from the ape,
Goat from sheep, it's not that deep.
Maybe sneaky for Vinter to turn sun to winter.
But that's the price we pay to live another day.
Even if only aardvarking in Lalalalalala Parking.
There's a streamer in the sky, a twinkle in God's eye.
A prism of the rainbow sent to Noah's table.

RADIO BROADCAST RETURNS.

RADIO:
In China, India, Asia, all across this sunny side of the globe, the temperature is one twenty five degrees Fahrenheit and climbing. The Chinese are mowing down those Japanese thirsting for knowledge. The Indian government are whacking the daylights out of the unenlightened. The Asian mob in Afghanistan are burning every building and store hoping that will quell the heat raging across the land. In the mountains the sheep and horses are stampeding the humans because the grass has wilted to mad salad. The seas have turned red and Japan has released its tanks of radioactive waste onto the land, into the

streams and ocean, across the asphalt. Like King Lear
says, My problem es su problema.

UFO's BUZZING THOSE WITH FLASHLIGHTS IN THE CITY.

GUIT:
There's a pilot over yonder pulling off a Honda.
This Charon is so bold to claim a wayward soul.
He is the boat on the Styx in which sinners sit,
Listening to the fell spell that coaxes Joe to hell.
Clamor and dissention mark travel to a new dimension.

DRUNK MAN:
Cheers, Mc Cartney. Give us a song.

GUIT:
Drink will be your downfall. Look for a mattress.

DRUNK GIRL:
Hey, I resemble that remark.

GUIT:
She's a tart and everybody's icing.

DRUNK GIRL:
Say that with a smile or come out fighting.

GUIT:
See. Ten beers later, no free speech. Only
tart peaches. Grumpy mountains, dry valleys.
Truffles.

ENTER COP WITH NIGHTSTICK.

COP:
Keep it moving. No loitering, mawdickers.

DRUNK GIRL:
What about chu, misfit?

DRUNKS AND COP MOVE ALONG.

GUIT:
When will something crazy happen?

HUGE BOULDER ROLLS ACROSS.
GUIT:
Free speech is hazardous, yes. I wanna tell
the gopher and hedgehogs, skunks, beaver, and
weasel, curb your tongue or you'll be aardvarking
in La La La Parking. Ants and termites on the
tongue--Ow! I'm gonna go out, get me some. La la la---

EXIT GUITAR PLAYER. ENTER DUDE AND SLUT
AMIDST AMBIENT STREET NOISES.

DUDE:
I am jonesing for some kona, a hand to soap my lufa.

SLUT:
Yo. Boomerang. Come back and pay me.

DUDE:
You waffled when you said you're over easy.
You're scrambled, pancake. Mabel syrup by
my fork.

SLUT:
You try the gods, you pay the tithe.

DUDE:
You smell the grave, you know she no babe.
Addioats, Kellog.

SLUT:
Get outta 'ere, drumroll. I can't hear myself fart.

EXIT DUDE. REENTER GUITAR PLAYER.

GUIT:
Hair so fiery eyes so bright brow cool as metal in the night; thoughts so wild hands of birds bombs and rockets are her words; ballet steps, looks that linger, tossed contempt from her fingers.

SINGER SITS. ENTER PRESIDENT AND SENATOR FRANK.

PREZ:
What does NASA say?

SEN:
It's a once-in-twenty-five-thousand-year event.

PREZ:
And we got tickets. Whoo hoo! What a concert. And no one forecast darkness, did they?

SEN:
Well—

PREZ:
Spill it, Hoover.

SEN:
My son-in-law.

PREZ
This is why we have tongues and pussies.

SEN:
To bring saline love to half the world?
The cunny linguist bet on a breakdown this week.

PREZ:
So the trillions I lost—

SEN:
In his pocket.

PREZ:
We could freeze his assets.

SEN:
And put on the steamer the Mob, the American
Indian Federation, Wall Street mavens, the BBB?
He's gottem all in his trousers. The Catholic
Church, the Treasury, the Salvation Army--pocket.

SLUT SLITHERS FORWARD.

SLUT:
Hey, sailor.

PREZ:
Just a minute.

EXIT PRESIDENT AND SENATOR FRANK.

SLUT:
I am the Queen of Darkness, holding your ticket to La La Parking—

EXIT SLUT. ENTER VENDOR.

VEN:
Flashlights. Fifty dollah. Flashlights. Gettem while they're lit. Flashlights.

EXIT VENDOR. ENTER KICKING ANTELOUPE WITH DAY WORKERS.

KICK:
Alright. Tonight: flashlights and booze. Tomorrow: aspirin, milk, and batteries. The next day: speed and No Doz. The day after: sandwiches, coats, blankets, rooms. Got that? Good. Don't lose your key to the hideout. Or your map.

WORKER ONE:
How long will our job last?

KICK:
Five days. Then when the ball starts rolling again, new contract. See ya then.

EXIT NIGHT WORKERS. ENTER SENATOR.

KICK:
Pops. How's tricks?

SEN:
Kicker. I don't know what to say.

KICK:
I don't hear, "I was wrong." Wrong to doubt
you. Wrong to put my own daughter in a helicopter.
Wrong to kiss up to executive power's dangers.
Wrong to trust the monster even as it devours
everything we see. Or, conversely, don't see.
The naked sky diver falling. Sleepy, bladder
full, semen caked, bothered.

SEN:
But--Congress--the White House--The Constitution!

KICK:
A sewing circle! The outhouse! Toilet paper!

EXIT KICKING ANTELOUPE. SLUT SCOOTS FORWARD.

SLUT:
Hey, Big Boy. Huge. Are you hot and bothered?

EXIT SENATOR IN A HUFF.

SLUT:
What'd I say? What'd I say? Damn it. Oh well.
Bring it on home, homeboys, to the Queen of Darkness.
At your service at La La Parking.

EXIT SLUT. REENTER SINGER WITH GUITAR.

GUIT:
Let her fly, let her fly, like a bird on the wind
and if you love her well, what are you still
doing here? Take a breath, paint the sky,
become the bay leaf of her mind, chase your
dream past sunrise and always hug her dear.
Kiss her sweet breath for she's the best and
stroke her downy chin, weave her spirit into
cloud as free as cherubim. Let her fly,
let her fly, like a tornado in the Spring--
and if you love her well drink her down and
never fear. Let her fly, let her fly, then
fall--fall--fall--between pokey butterfly wings.

EXIT SINGER WITH GUITAR. ENTER MADMAN.

MAD:
It's a conspiracy. The commies. The Baptists.
The Senators. The Lakers. The Cowboys. Night!

ENTER MAD GIRL.

M GIRL:
So many plots a graveyard; so much tar a highway,
with lots of frontage leading to La La Parking.
Nearby the drive in. One world order, no substitutions.

MAD:
Uncage my kit, you can't tame her! Unchain midnight:
the tigress that stripes my zebra soul. Go on, dig
that hole, warden. Clod that wipes my striped hole.
Nut-uh.

M GIRL:
Get your torch outta my face, freakazoid. We can no more share the divine light than we can slake the desert with hot blood. Oh no!

REENTER SINGER. EXIT MADMAN.

GUIT:
Few lose your ticket, there's no exit, Madam X, from wooden Indians.

REENTER KICKING ANTELOUPE.

KICK:
Hey all you fence straddlers, listen up. If you buy into our plan for a new earth I'll give you an IOU for ten grand. If the plan don't pan out, you can sleep on my couch until we recover the cushions.

REENTER MADMAN.

MAD:
Bedbugs of the world, unite!

KICK:
Dance your shoes off in this fantasy.

MAD:
We are the Big Dogs, we are the biting fleas.

KICK:
Come on and join the party, there's only success and bounty.

MAD:
Uncork these loaded bottles—

KICK:
Of the wines of enlightenment.

MAD:
Wanna meet a mover 'n' shaker? Come and kiss
this sweet potater. Hey, don't knock over the
salt shaker. I gotta go. See ya later.
Tell the world, Stop you haters! Come and kiss
this sweet potater. The earth's filled with
nymphs and satyrs gnawin' on that sweet potater.

M GIRL:
If I hand you gold. Sweet land of mystery,
blessed by the dollar bill.

MAD:
Like our foreskins wallopped it. Grab it,
feel it, freak it. Yeah, baby.

M GIRL:
Quit. My mascara. My implants. Myopia.

MAD:
What's so grand about your opening?

M GIRL:
The glitter, the glamour, the glitz.

MAD:
No wonder your name's Glinda. For your
glittoral blisters, sister.

M GIRL:
If I had a man for every comedian I've
eaten I could fashion a stool big enough
for you to sit in, Tool.

MAD:
A sit-in's for protestors. You're a riot.
Anarchy! Right right right. Widdershins.

MAD MAN EXITS TO THE LEFT.

M GIRL:
There's nothing right or left with no
traffic cop to bend Moriah's earlobe. (whistles)
EXIT MAD GIRL RIGHT. ENTER MARCHING BAND
WITH
BATON TWIRLING BAND LEADER WOMAN IN FRONT.

BAND:
Join us in our brass parade. We will troop
till break of day.

BAND EXITS. LIGHTS FLASHING, A WRECKER DRIVER
ROLLS ONTO STAGE.

KICK:
What's the problem, officer?

DRIVER:
I'm not ever off duty nor a pig. The Seven
Twenty Four is my gig. Looking for looted
and trashed vehicles.

KICK:
Where's the five oh?

DRIVER:
In their den of thieves counting down to
retirement. Afraid of cockroaches, coyotes,
vermin. You call them; they won't answer.

KICK:
That's stupid.

DRIVER:
If you need seventy five dollah finders fee,
we're one block ovah from Maria's Tortas.
By the Airport long term lot.

KICK:
Gotcha, mockingbird. You got a boat?

DRIVER:
Funny thing, I just happen—

KICK:
You're gonna need it before the night is over.

TOWING DRIVER DRIVES OFF. BRASS BAND RETURNS.

BAND:
Dead end street. And I thought the drum roll
was for the quick and the dead.

KICK:
Someone stole the sign for scrap. Like shooting
vagrants to feed the watchdog and her pups.

BRASS BAND GOES OFF IN ANOTHER DIRECTION.

KICK:
These are the days of love and weeping.
Breaking the chains of dogs and keepers.

ENTER SINGER WITH GUITAR. EXIT KICKER.

GUIT:
Hey, catchy, kingfish. These are the nights
of froth and madness, bring some salt to spice
your battery. Take a tent and sleeping bag.
Every Clark has to rest whenever he has to.

ENTER WOMAN CHASED BY A MAN.

MAN:
Hey, all I—

WOMAN:
Oh no you don't—

GUIT:
Not every Pudge can hit a homer. Leave it to
the fist of ugly Romeo.

REENTER MAN BEING CHASED BY WOMAN WITH A BASEBALL BAT.

MAN:
Life is a bitch—

WOMAN:
--and so are you.

EXIT MAN.

WOMAN:
He drains the shadows of their ire and whips
pinned pupils into the Nile. The curl of his
forehead Egyptian god asks the question as she
nods; a vein of fury on his temple beats to a
refrain wild yet sturdy. Black leather in
creeky jazz snare wrinkle noses and the stares.
Grab the vacant mic before he howls a grizzlie
shout out from his bowels. Instead of poetry
or even horns his hand tosses drumstick storms.
Soon the jacket carpets the floor as the beaten
oven begs for more. Each shake more encaptivating
due to the flowers salivating. Flashes of thunder
ply the mob and the collective hive throbs.
Buzzing to the honey of his sticks the ant army
arches its kicks. A brazen vampire come to life
where every female accepts his bite. Then the
drumsticks--all but broken--sent to the masses
hot and smoking: two stakes 'mongst the statuary
of the vampire sanctuary. Their gaze a cry of
anguish where their poor souls languish. They're
drained, cracked China cups holding onto their
bruised cuts, seeping.

EXIT WOMAN TOSSING BAT. BAT TURNS INTO A REAL BAT, FLIES AWAY. ENTER MEN IN BLACK WITH MAD MAN IN STRAIGHT JACKET
BEING HUSTLED ALONG FORCEFULLY.

GUIT:
What did you do, citizen, to deserve this rough—

MAD:
I escaped from Cyronic Incorporated. They know I'm the only one that can bring the Rat Pack back to life.

MIB ONE:
Enough of the interview. Move it. Tell it to the judge.

MAD MAN:
Judge, hell. More like Mr. Wallaby and Joey.

GUIT:
Do you need a lawyer, amigo?
MAD MAN:
I am too far gone to run. At the limit of my strength. A horseshoe thrown by Orion a-following my bent.

SINGER STRUMS ALONG WITH THE MAD MAN. EXIT MIB AND MAD MAN. ENTER MAD GIRL.

M GIRL:
Have you seen my cat?

GUIT:
Um, meow.

M GIRL:
Here, puppa wuppa. Come to Mommy.

EXIT MAD GIRL WITH THE SINGER'S FLASHLIGHT.

GUIT:
There goes the Alexandria Lighthouse. Pillars of Hercules next.

ENTER AARDVARKERS AND FEINERS.

FEINER:
Hooking through the neighborhood. Where I swing life is good. Every pleasure at my finger, steaming high heeled opera singer. Free the bird and grease the palm, I won't do you any harm. Whistle diddle shake that wattle, battleship that wins the battle. Look for Snooky to play hooky, need your dough to bake my cookies. You are shy but I am brash. Snap those digits when I stride to stallion your midnight ride. Swaying from the stop sign pole, separating miser from his gold. Cooking beans in a pot, let me see whatcha gots. Hooking through the cool snow drifts, giving all the stiffs a lift. For the razor meets the leather, in the clover and hot Heather.

AARD:
Are you looking for a boost, a head long rush? Tired of choking in the weeds? Try angel dust. You can eat it, snort it, juice it, enema it, swallow in it, shoot it, pop it, beat it in your eggs pounding the wife—

FEINER:
Idiot! Move.

AARD:
Drink it, hoover it, goose it, rocket.

FEINER:
`PCP's a pain. ICE rules the day.

AARD:
It's night time, the right time to get higher
'n' higher.

ENTER MORE MEN IN BLACK.

MIB TWO:
Alright, you scrunge suckers. Pull over.
We're looking for some warm cats, otherwise
known as catatonic boobies. They're not in
their right minds. We pay one bill per cat.
They have to be warm and breathing. No broken
bones or organs. Skull fractures okay but they
must be recent. Got that? Good. Here's a
flyer in case of short term memory loss et cetera.

MEN IN BLACK MOVE OFF CALLING FOR MORE HOT CATS.

GUIT:
I'm broke as a stone in a gravel truck. But
I'm ain't turning in cadavers for billionaires
to fetch roller coaster rides around on.

AARD:
You don't have to have mo money. You just
gotta shake the monstrosity.

FEINER:
Hey, we're legit. My dad's a councilman.
We squash writs. Come see us. Let's go, Angelo.

AARD:
Ha ha ha ha.
EXIT FEINER.

AARD:
How did the logo go before the dremels of justice struck? To protect the witch and serve the kettle. Teased by mulberry teats on a float. What is the lesson I am teaching me? Guardian Demon, answer truly. Baptized by the fire of heaven I perk until I'm blind. Echo in the cup of tarnished silver, gild the picture composing Buddha. Streak through the red sand storm. As soon as the cash runs out, so did she. I looked in the looking glass for a sight of Alice but she's past the suburbs, half way to Dallas. It's a happy thought to keep a wad in my boot.

EXIT AARDVARKER.

GUIT:
How'd this glass pipe get in my pocket? Ow. Hot!

REENTER MAD GIRL.

M GIRL:
Hot pockets of my soul; steal a flashlight, let it go. Ever randy as a goat, you're the captain of my boat.

GUIT:
If I'm a captain I'm Ahab. Cause this great white whale is stuck between decks. And I can't pull my lower deck outta its jaws long enough to harden my resolve. What? No I don't have another torch.

M GIRL:
I've taken a shine to your guitar. My knight in shining armor. Shawn Amore.

GUIT:
Ach, your lips tast of corn syrup. Who switched the formula? Cornspearacy! Cornspearacy! This net--
Hey, is Annette your name?

M GIRL:
It could be. Once I was an astronette, Glen of the Strong Arms. And moon rocks.

GUIT:
Annette is trying to entrap me. Cornspearacy!

M GIRL:
Dude, your flashlight's running low on batteries. Recharge: thirty skins.

GUIT:
You better leggo the armadillo, Annette, and avoid the semi beeping in front of you.

M GIRL:
You're funny. Humor's disarming, and I'm Venus. Venus de Milo, at mile zero on the highway. Red light.

GUIT:
You are so appropo. But I must say No.

M GIRL:
So, Dude. What's happening? Why the depression?

GUIT (singing):
He killed a man his pockets full sent a soul
back to the pool; the good die young on the
hot seat, the good die young. He was watching
video games when a copper bullet called his name;
the good die young on the X-Box, the good die young.
Oh why? She never shouda answered the phone for
soon a semi crushed her bones. The good die young
on their Apples, the good die young. Aye yai!
The young miss grabbed a stick and felt the fire
of a viper kiss; the good die young at the camp
site, the good die young. They were swaying to
the music when the final chord brought down cherubim;
the good die young at a concert, the good die young. Ow!
He plucked the rubber from the wire at the pole,
ate that fryer all alone; the good die young on a
pole vault, the good die young. Shanghai'ed by
sparky-o. That's right, scrapper, the good die young.

ENTER KICKING ANTELOUPE WITH KIDS HOLDING BUNDLES OF NEWSPAPERS.

KICK:
Get you copy of my vision hot off the presses. Get informed.

M GIRL:
What does it say?

KID ONE:
Everything will be dark for five days. Then here comes a mini-Ice Age.

M GIRL:
Great. My coat's at the pawn shop. My knickers are at Ralph's. My boots are in the garage. And my scarf is being tended by mice.

ENTER DRUNKEN MOB OF TIPPLERS.

DRUNK:
There's no last call to be frantic. Guzzler down like the Titanic. Muzzler, Highbrow, and Mozeltoff yanked the tank and wanked a bomb. Why didn't Hitler explode the comet that brought us down this road? Well, he had such a short fuse his dynamite was so old.

EXIT GROUP OF DRUNKS.

GUIT:
The clouds whisper in cherub speak, the time is near and sight is weak; we do not know but still we seek the palace in the mists of Eternity. The clouds whisper to the mountain peaks; the vision is clear yet sight is weak. The time is now but our plight is bleak; dressed up in the Bermuda shorts of Destiny.

REENTER DRUNKS.

DRUNK:
Follow us, everybody, into the lobby. Free popcorn and hot dogs, by golly. Mustard, relish, sour kraut,

cheese. Cholestrol goodies to bring Kareem to his knees.

DRUNKS EXIT AGAIN.

GUIT:
Do you smell that?

M GIRL:
Are you feeling curry?

DRUNK OFFSTAGE.

DRUNK:
The butter--the butter--the butter---

M GIRL:
But, but. Will you love me in the morning? Will you
kiss me by the hedge?

GUIT:
Can't you help me raise the tattered flag? I'm
at half mast because my libido so morbid.

M GIRL:
Kareem, Kareem, Kareem, I don't go down that street.

GUIT:
Who's the raker didn't pave the alley?
I gotta smoke the rod to toot rad Sally. Sally,
Sally, grab the blanket.

M GIRL:
Why?

GUIT:
Cause we're headed out for Look Out Point.

M GIRL:
Well, I declare. I can barely get this
Dodge in gear. It's shifty.

GUIT:
Never you worry, I've got the courage to spice
a balladeer.

M GIRL:
What if it floods?

GUIT:
We'll bring a towel and Tidy Wipes. A rubber
bed and some latex gloves.

M GIRL:
Urgency. You're like a Boy Scout, I swear.

GUIT:
Gimme your hand and I'll take you there.
If this is Doomsday don't miss a chance.
For one last fling; a wild romance.

M GIRL:
Wipe off the blackboard with a black bird.
Put on sunglasses and a welder's hoodie.
If we be daid the worms inherit the goodies.
What's that noise? It's too quiet somehow.

GUIT:
It don't-- The nightingale whispers.

ANGRY VOICES. A CROWD SCREAMING. WATER RUSHES IN. REENTER KICKING ANTELOUPE WITH KIDS IN RUBBER RAFTS.

KICK:
Alright, you lubbers, let's get to work.
Unchuck the nuts from the tires. Use the
inner tubes as floats. Grab five gallon buckets.
The logs that once were trash, pure titanium.

GIRL ONE:
Get your hands on your own rubber duckies; this
one's mine!

GIRL ONE BEATS OFF SWIMMER WITH WET TOWEL. OLD LADY DOG PADDLING BEHIND.

SWIMMER:
You oar! Pond jumper. Snake oil.

OLD LADY:
What's happening? I can't swim a lick.

KICK:
Who will be the frog man and twist a few nuts?

ENTER GAY GUY AND OTHERS.

GAY GUY:
Don't get me started. I'm a better art
student and film buff. Teevee buff. History
buff. Anything buff, Butch; I'm your man,
and honey chile; alternate, flip flop, Love.

RENTER DRUNKS.

DRUNK:
Oh Catalina, cry me a river.

DRUNK FLOATS AWAY BUOYED BY WINE BOTTLES AND BLOWN UP RUBBERS. ENTER DYKE AND BUTCH MAN.

DYKE:
Are you the Dutch boy got us into this mess?

BUTCH:
Look what we have 'ere. A ball of snakes and a
huddle of meteors. You got raspberry jam on yer chin,
sweetheart.

DYKE:
Quit misbehavin'. Go nail your savior, cross-dresser.

BUTCH:
He was aborted at the clinic, sadly. Now
the whole fajita steak festival is hurting.
All the cutlets are crying. Rusty as nails.

GAY GUY:
If you're so manly you'll come in handy.
Remove some tires. Make yourself useful.

BUTCH:
I can't. My back.

GAY GUY RIPS BUTCH'S T-SHIRT.

GAY GUY:
My oh my, look't all dem hickeys.

BUTCH:
No, no. They're bites from the leaches teeming,
uh, in my backyard swamp. (pause) God's
truth. I ketch bullfrogs for French cafes.
And the Gay Paree cookoff.

GAY GUY:
I'll buy that for a blow job. Keep up the
good fork, Tiny.

KICK:
Someone, please. We need floatation before
the waters rise more.

KID TWO:
This must be what the New Age was pointing to.

GAY GUY:
Read for me: I'm dyslexic.

KID TWO:
The Water Bearer. It's only temporary. Bear
with the water's implied.

GAY GUY:
Makes sense. I'll be your cub, Daddy Bear.
I done lost my slippers 'n' drawers. I can't
get much barer can I? Just think: we're just
a skinny dip away from salvation. Praise the

Lord.

DYKE:
Sounds like a sing-along. I was brought into the world with nothing.

GUIT:
Oh. Oh. And now I'm rich as a bitch can be.

GAY GUY:
And the world just keeps huffing and puffing while we ride the waves of Californee.

DYKE:
Don't say that life is cruel and flighty.

GUIT:
Feel a stroke from every bloke out on the street.

GAY GUY:
I'm not sayin' you don't have a nice hiney; but if the tide deeps coming I'll lose my weenie in the rip tide or hell, any Rip Wastrel that comes along, or not so long either way I'm game. Just so I gets to eat!

BUTCH:
Kum bai yah! Kum bai yah!

DYKE:
Don't overload the jacuzi. You lose if you snooze. Jasus, Dude! Hands!

BUTCH:
These spiders can't be controlled. They're growing webs between the fingers. I'm making the Aquarian age man, man.

KICK:
Man the boats and guide the rudder. Everyone's about to meet his mudder.

GAY GUY:
Great. I wanna give Moms a big fat kiss and a stinging slap for birthing a monstrosity. Arrrhl!

GEL:
Oh Lord we need more krackens.

BOY:
And cheese wiz to go with'em.

BUTCH:
Reach into my pocket. Pull the octopus off my eel.

GAY GUY:
Squid would be better served. With habenero.

BUTCH:
Shark! Shark!

EVERYONE SCATTERS.

BOY:
What's that thing that goes boink in the night?

GEL:
It's a green sea turtle giving the polo team
a fright. I'm safe. I'm safe. As long as I
got my plastic crucifix.

KICKING ANTELOUPE AND HIS TWO KIDS SWIM OFF.
REENTER MAD MAN, MIB, AND J EDGAR HOOVER.
EXCEPT HOOVER IS
SEVEN FOOT TALL. AND BLACK BELOW THE
NECKLINE.

HOOVER:
Arrh. Haah. Nooo. Back to nothing.

MIB ONE:
What is he saying?

MAD MAN:
You want me to interpret a corpse's thoughts.
Nosirree.

HOOVER:
Worms. Drugs. Mammaries.

MAD MAN:
I tole you we should have reawakened Jimi
Hendrix or Janis. What a waste of a good body.

MIB ONE:
You don't get to decide. Senator Frank is
the head honcho, no pun intended.

HOOVER:
Black cats. Roman candles. Artillery. M-80's.

MAD MAN:
You see. His brain's been too long in the dark. Explosions and fireworks. Why am I being hijacked like this? I want to go back to my goldfish pond and koi.

HOOVER STRIKES THE MIB. THE MIB RESTRAIN HIM.

HOOVER:
Murph. Slaw. Booger wooger. Halt malted. Gooseberries!

MAD MAN:
Why did we resurrect this moron? Huh?

MIB ONE:
The electricity was going. It was our last best chance and a body was available.

HOOVER:
Bugs. Cubs. Mashed potatoes. It's all snooky!

MAD MAN:
See? He is worse off than me, a defrocked doctor of implant and repair surgery. Shoot the zombie and be done with it. I'm—

MIB ONE:
Oh no you don't. You stay right here. We got a wire on you so you can be found no problem.

HOOVER:
Bella. Bass amphibian. Pooky.

MAD MAN:
See? Sex on the brain and cooties too.
What about all the other heads about to rot
at room temperature? We could have Bobby or
Marilyn.

MIB ONE:
Again, above my pay grade. Let's take him
back to the holding tank. Work on another
cadaver and unfreeze another hellhound on the world.

EXIT MIB, MAD MAN, WITH HOOVER'S RESURRECTED
BODY UNDER RESTRAINT. ZIPPING AND ZAPPING AS
MICROMETEORS HIT THE
WATER.

GAY GUY:
Oh Sheila and Madame X's pantaloons, who's
shooting at us? Who's throwing this Syrian
bullet ballet?

DYKE:
Get outta my butt, Pinocchio impersonator.
Can't turn my back on you.

DUDE:
Are you calling me a bottom feeder. Please,
sister, don't bottle up your anger. Let it
bleed. Mani hara Omaha.

DYKE:
Don't blame it on the liquor, goosey lips.
The insane autour of these things asks you
not to get too near. Lest I spur you.

DUDE:
You're no rooster. Don't flap your feathers,
Hen. Shed your crystalis, Soma. Let's wing
it to Panther Hall. Hear Nitty Gritty Dirt Band.

KICKER:
These mad gods are shedding hot tears and they
fall not far from our beaten hearts. Watch out.

OLD LADY:
We have our poverty and we have our dreams.
Take the dream away from the beggar and you
set cool death in the baroque gutter.

SWIMMER:
When there is nothing left to lose except more
suffering, what do you supply the demon? You
can't steal perfume from a corpse. How can you
punish a rock?

REENTER GEL AND BOY WITH A BLACK GARBAGE
BAG. ALSO A PRIEST WITH MONSTRONCE WITH
HOST
INSIDE. PLUS THE BRASS
BAND PLAYING.

GEL:
Look what we found. Old submarine sandwiches.
All tuna.

KICKER:
Bread. Albacore. Come get yer loaves 'n'
fishes right here. Cheap. Just sign over
the mineral rights to your souls.

GEL:
Fish for souls. Sole for minerals.

BOY:
Crust for crawlers. Swim on ovah. Hurry before they get soggy.

GEL:
Don't apologize for being solly. Hitch up your lips and your britches, bitches. Tuna for puma. Warm the cockles of yer esophagus.

MAN:
Where do I sign?

KICKER
See how easy it is, kids? Easy as shooting fish in a barrel.

GAY GUY:
Who wants my John Hancock?

DUDE:
Hungay.

GAY GUY:
You've been saving that up to flood my foyer.

DYKE:
Quit stepping all over my fishing lines, worm. I gotta feed this tapeworm. And you thought it was a bambino. Heya, I'm no Prima Donna. My tag is Barney Sloffalottaguts.

DUDE:
Bitch needs to go on a troglodiet.

MAN:
Hey. Look what you did. You made me feed
my whopper to the flounder and sting ray.
Ma'am, I need another sandwich.

BOY:
Sorry, only one per sailor. But if you row
your dingy over to Cuba...

REENTER MIB ON INNER TUBES AND MAD MAN
TOTING A STEAMER TRUNK.

MIB ONE:
And you thought you were Cardinal Richelieu
hiding your gelt.

MAD MAN:
I don't know where the diamonds and gold is.
I swear. I'm hungry. I'm tired.

MIB TWO:
Keep those heads dry you moron!

MAD MAN:
Sorry.

GEL:
No whining!

MIB TWO:
I'll say. These floating tires are a life

saver. Har har har.

MIB ONE:
We oughta troll for marlin.

MAD MAN:
I'm no magician. The landmarks are like
a California renter.

MIB ONE:
If I don't see a payday, it's time for
a deep sea dive.

MAD MAN:
You can't do that. The Geneva Convention.

MIB TWO:
She's out shopping for basic woman's boxing
gloves to use to fight for her riots.

MAD MAN:
Oh, oh! Stop, turn left. No rights.
Now I remember.

MIB ONE:
You're gonna lose more'n a digit, Yakuza.
Get your mind right and soon. Unless we
hear clear, concise directions. Sabes?

MAD MAN:
The bell tower. Find the bell tower.
The stash is in the walls.

MIB TWO:
Finally, punk.

MIB ONE:
Was that so hard? Hands up. Extended.

MAD MAN:
If you drown me I'll return. Curse you.
Tape open Doomsday's Door. Haunt your bones.
Scare your family all night.

MIB TWO:
This night never ends does it?

MIB AND MAD MAN EXIT.

BOY:
But if you can bring us the hand of a
corpse---

MAN:
I won't waste my chance.

GEL:
That's so sick.

EXIT MAN WITH KNIFE BETWEEN HIS TEETH.

GEL:
Give us a thumbprint as payment. Loaves
'n' fishes for your tushes.

BOY:
If you are not satisfied, eat your meal—

GEL:
Just sign over your doubtful soul.

BOY:
--and burp a while. In the flux of your stomach you will feel Doomsday coming with the seventh sealant, protein.

GAY GUY:
It tastes so good.

DYKE:
I love a foot long between friends. Yum.

KICKER:
Eat of your ignorance. Join the dance.

OLD LADY:
Who are you people anyway?

KICKER:
The Soul Team. Gathering loose souls for one last fandango. Sweeping up the crumbs and the thumbs. Hitch hiking across the firmament.

OLD LADY:
What's your goal?

GEL:
Three hundred maybe.

KICKER:
Nirvana.

BOY:
It doesn't matter. Live. Eat. Breathe.
Gather the sheaves with others.

MAN RETURNS WITH HAND ATOP HIS HEAD.

MAN:
Here, here. Almost lost my shiv.
DYKE:
Can't get to Nirvana without Shiva, Ganesh.

KICKER:
Sorry. Wrong hand. We need the right one.
See? This is the left one.

MAN:
Right?

KICKER:
Right.

EXIT MAN GRUMBLING.

GEL:
Who's gonna know?

KICKER:
Ah. We'll use some clay to invert the mark.
Good as done.

GEL:
Loaves 'n' fishes, come on, folks. Give
an imprint. Watch your swirls at work.

OLD LADY:
Why does each imprint box say Marco Diablo?

KICKER:
It's Latin for Hot Ink. That's the name of
the silicon valley soul processors. They
extract every useful mineral. Turn man into
a pay phone. I can already hear those coins
clinking. Cha-ching!

GEL:
Come 'n' get yer loaves 'n' fishes, do not
smirk, ditch your sneakers, or be dismissive.
Or you'll be wishin' for Babe's hot kitchen.

BOY:
How many do we have?

GEL:
How full is a Beast's belly? Keep goin'.
BOY:
No shortage of flailing bodies.

GEL:
Quit with the oddball questions. Heya, lumberjack.

ENTER SINGER GUY AND MAD GIRL.

GUIT:
Where ya goin', Paul, wit dat edge?

M GIRL:
Give me Liberty or give me an air mattress.

GEL:
Where'd you get those floats, Bub?

GUIT:
The Sail Shop, Sally. Anchors aweigh.
It's a long, it's a long, it's a long
way to go--because dawn stalls.

BRASS BAND ON FLOATS PLAYS ALONG.

SALLY:
Your chopsticks tickle my snare drum. We need
a banjo and fiddle.

GUIT:
You're right. Follow that brass calliope.

SINGER AND SALLY EXIT ON LOUNGE FLOATS. RAIN FALLS. AND SLEET. THUNDER CLASHES

KICKER:
Let me sleep a little while longer, Orpheus.

BOY:
Damn YMCA.

GEL:
My bunk bed's a board of Bowie knives. Sucks!
Dad, what are we--I'm confused. My breath is
noxious as a sewer. Are we being used?

BOY:
I can't feel my cranberries or Joey Dolittle.

GEL:
Why are we looking for a few good hands again?
And the voter registration stuff?

KICKER:
Don't worry about it. Think of it as stirring
zombie stew for your sweetie.

GEL:
Right. And I'm the princess of Whales to your
prince of darkness.

REENTER MAD MAN WITH A ZOMBIE WITH
SHAKESPEARE'S HEAD ON A BALLERINA'S BODY.
THEY ARE CARRYING FIVE GALLON
BUCKETS WITH HOLES CUT INTO THE MIDDLE OF
THEM.

MAD MAN:
We're back.

SHAKES:
When the tar, when the glue, when the paint
buckets escape the trash bin—

MAD MAN:
We dodged the government goons. What do you
want to know?

KICKER:
I almost got your order filled. For the you-know.

MAD MAN:
Gotcha. Anything to aid a seeker, a fellow
traveler, a Buddha belly polisher.

SHAKES:
Paint cover the sto', I will flow from blue
to green and never ask for—

KICK:
I'd do whatever it is you want to revive my
lost love.
SHAKES:
Beware the eyes of October, they have such—

MAD MAN:
Oh I can do the impossible. Get those forms
filled out so I can have a quorum of souls
to spring me out of Hades later. I really
hate hot weather. Mom was a devil worshipper.
So--yeah.

KICKER:
Any final thoughts?

MAD MAN:
Just keep on paddling. Let's go, Billie Jean.

SHAKES:
All hair, Quackbeth. Cornspearacy, Monsanto.

GEL:
And Fritos for all.

MAD MAN:
Mellonie, Maria, and Boo went off to see the zoo...

EXIT MAD MAN AND SHAKESPEARE BALLERINA PULLING COYOTE AND HAWK HALLOWEEN DISGUISES. BEHIND THEM ENTERS MIB WITH BLACK FEATHER CLOAKS. MAD MAN AND SHAKESPEARE BALLERINA BOPPING THEIR RUBBER HEADS TO UNKNOWN MUSIC.

MIB ONE:
Where are they? I heard voices. What did you do with the scoundrels?

KICK:
I poured them into a flask and sold them for gin. Come on, guys. Let's punt these sandwiches to some taco barge.

MIB SEARCH THE SURROUNDINGS. KICKING ANTELOUPE AND HIS TWINS EXIT. ENTER CANOE RENTAL OUTFIT, MAN WITH A BUNCH OF CANOES IN TOW. MIB EXIT.

CANOE:
Canoes for rent. Rent your canoes. Keep your feet dry.

SUDDENLY, A FLAMING METEOR DEMOLISHES CANOE,
RENTER AND HIS CANOE. A KID SWIMS UP. HE SLAPS THE WATER TO
DISPERSE THE BUBBLES AND SMOKE. HE DIVES FOR MR CANOE. HE RESURFACES.

KID TWO:
Wow! Did that really happen? Hey. Guy!

KID TWO HOPS INTO SPARE CANOE.

KID TWO:
Damn!! Canoes for sale. All offers
considered. Canoes for sale or rent.
Get them while they last.

ENTER A PASSEL OF YOUNGSTERS ON SWIM FLOATS,
BIKE INNER TUBES, CAR TIRE TUBES, FLOATIES,
ZIPLOCK BAGS, GALLON
CANS, FOAM STAFFS, SWANS, NET BAGS OF RUBBER
DUCKIES. THEY ARE TIED TOGETHER BY ROPES.

GIRL TWO:
Hey, Tim. If you're an instant millionaire,
put your posse to work. Banga trabajo, Jefe!

BOYZ:
Spread the wealth, Tim Can. Come on, Gordo.

ENTER OLD WOMAN FLOATING ON SKID PALLETS
WITH HER OLD MAN.

OLD WOMAN:
I want a canoe but I don't know how to operate
it. Got cash and jewelry.

TIM:
No problemo. I have galley slaves to man
the oars. Second mate Gabby.

GABBY:
You do? That was a quick promotion. I've been proposed to; at last. Yes, dear?

TIM:
Yes! I love free enterprise. Okay, get Spud and Meatball to help the lady to her seat.

GABBY:
You heard the Captain.

SPUD:
A tin captain.

GABBY:
Whatever. Get your sausage fingers in that pizza dough. Mush!

TIM:
The Rolex, the tennis bracelet and this ring. Another happy customer. Canoes! Canoes! Complete with old tars who work for—

SPUD:
We don't work for no peanuts, Cappy.

GABBY:
The normal adjusted wage.

OLD WOMAN:
Watch it. That way, young man.

MEATBALL:
It's been a year since Camp Bowie, lady.

OLD WOMAN:
I trust you. Here. Have a candy bar.

SPUD:
Adios, sugar. I'm gone exploring.

GABBY:
Oh, flush it. You one-time loser.

TIM:
Canoes. Flexible payment plans. We hand over canoe, then you go on cruise. The Princess Lion Cruise Company.

GABBY:
You got too many canoes to be safe. Any bandito could hit you and hijack them at any time.

TIM:
So? I'm new at this.

GABBY:
Put a guard in every boat. Use some soap in your sponge! It's gonna be a long--long--long--long night until dawn calls.

TIM:
Who's the boss here anyways?

GABBY:
Canoes. Canoes for rent or sale. Hey, you guys. Hop into these empty canoes. Hold onto your floaties just in case. Don't be blue, tip a canoe. Wanna know

wat's new? Adorable canoes. Paddle
through your troubles.

ENTER THUGS.

THUG ONE:
Can I test drive one?

THUG TWO:
Yeah, you know. Test paddle.

GABBY:
Okay. Sure, there you go. Touch it. As long
as you don't get us wet, Mr. Seaman.

TIM:
Great ride. Nice lines. Good mileage.
Stops on a diamond. What more could you
ask for? Let's see your wad of dinero.

THUG TWO:
Hey, how about a little credit. We're
short. Just swam across the bar ditch.
How about twenty dollah now and—

TIM:
Guys! Guys! Gather round. A wet
twinkee will only buy one game of--
the board game's pivotal--gang?

ALL THE CANOES GATHER AROUND THUGS.

ALL KIDS:
Whack-a-mole'!

ALL THE KIDS WHACK THE THUGS GOOFY.

GABBY:
You know where can take those Kibbles
'n' Bits, Tom and Jerry? The cat house.
Buy yourself a dose of Mariposa Gonorrhea..

THUGS:
You whores!

GABBY:
Thanks for the endorsement. So now you
can go funk everyone you meet that you
just got beaten off for free by a pack
of dry whores renting and selling gnus.
Canoes! Canoes! Buy them or fight us
until you're blue, warthog.

TIM:
We don't believe in charity, filanders.
So take your philantrophy of bruises
across the wet-lands.

GABBY:
Shiners and whiners, spread the word.

EXIT THUGS, GRUMBLING AND GESTURING AND
GRIMACING. ENTER SCIENTISTS IN TWO ZODIACS.
THEY ROLL IN, TURN OFF
THEIR ENGINES.

SCI ONE:
Hey, guys and Amazon leader. You want to
do some science for Uncle Sam while making

a treasure chest full of cash?

ALL KIDS:
Ah ya ha, yeah.

SCI ONE:
Okay, here's these compasses. Here's your
retainers also. Everyone split up---we
got p and b sandwiches to hold you over.
Go out and see if anyone can find true
North. You see, because of this darkness,
true North is invisible and we don't know why.
We just want to find it again. Bring it on
home. Meet us back here in let's say, eight
hours. All clear? Alright. Good luck
voyagers.

KIDS:
Swell. Yes! Wonderful. Who'da thunk it?
Damn it!

CANOES DISPERSE. SCIENTISTS CONTINUE
ZODIACING. ENTER JET SKI WITH SCUBA DIVER.
DIVER SIGNALS TO OTHER DIVERS
ON OTHER JET SKIS WHO CONGREGATE. ALL THESE
GUYS ARE ASIANS.

JET SKI:
All clear. Keep a keen look-out. No stragglers.
We're on a mission, soldiers.

A MINI-SUBMARINE SURFACES.

JET SKI:
Perimeter. Watch out for coast guard.
Push outsiders away. Be firm.

SUB CAPTAIN:
Good work, Lieutenant. Find a hill to
plant our flag. Be quick about it.

LIEU:
There's nothing here but a Macy's sign

SUB CAPTAIN:
Keep looking. We're on the leading edge
of the invasion. Strike with might. We're
so so close. Push on. Go!
LIEU:
You got it, sir. Should we shoot to maim
or to kill?

SUB CAPTAIN:
Use your discretion. No quarter, no Bama,
no Georgia.

REENTER THUGS WITH GUNS AND
REINFORCEMENTS.

THUG ONE:
Look at these scavengers. They brought in
their mules and burros. Waste the amarillos.

THUGS AND INVASION FORCE COLLIDE. GUNS GO
OFF.
JET SKIS RUN. SUB DIVES. THUGS BITE THE BULLETS.

THUG TWO:
I hate crapital investment on a shoestring budget. Ow.

THUGS DROWN.

THUG ONE:
We can't roll over for orphans. Scum.
SUBMARINE RESURFACES GUNS BLAZING. A MISSLE HITS SUB. IT DISAPPEARS. REENTER SCIENTISTS.

SCI ONE:
Fricking MIT scrappers. We're out-manned. But not for long. Regroup, Marines!

ZODIAC RETREATS, DROPPING DEPTH CHARGES. CANOES WITH THE KIDS RETURN. THEY SHOOT OFF ROMAN CANDLES AND
FLARES. THEY HURL BLACKCAT STRINGS. THEY SET OFF BOTTLE ROCKETS. THEY TOSS SMOKE BOMBS AND GIANT FIREWORKS.

GABBY:
Don't let them form a turtle. Or we'll get waxed. Blast'em. Hit'em hard. Don't lettem gain the Macy's sign. Let chaos rein!

TIM:
This is the Wild West on cancer, steroids, acid, ecstasy, cheese. Get outta my sights, Viking. Go rape and pillage Compton. This is our hood, hairball.

MEATBALL:
We gotcha back, Cap. In spite of the sugar
and three-D wages.

GABBY:
Who were those losers? They acted like
Hell's Angels on PCP and crack, wine and Jack.

REENTER KICKING ANTELOUPE DRESSED AS
NEPTUNE
WITH A DOLPHIN POWERED FLOAT. HIS KIDS ARE
TOSSING FISH AND
SHRIMP TO THE MARINE LIFE, AND MARDI GRAS
NECKLACES TO THE OTHER YOUNGSTERS.

KICK:
Keep the faith, Swabbies and Nymphs. We're
almost there. The world spin is reversing.
I can feel its current. My GPS is spinning
like a Daytona winner on a hot-wired pavement.

TIM:
Say, who are you anyway?

KICK:
I'm Neptune the god of the waning age. See
my trident. It's empowered to light up the
seven seas until the New Age starts.

REENTER MAD MAN WITH BUFFALO MAIDEN'S
ZOMBIE DOUBLE. ALSO RENTER MAN WHO LOST HIS
LUNCH COVERED WITH DOZENS
OF CUT OFF HANDS TIED TO HIS ARMS AND EARS,
ARRIVES THE OTHER WAY.

MAN:
Here I am, back from the dead. Ready to trade
my recyclables for bread.

MAD MAN:
What, is the man lunatic?

KICK:
Ah, there you are with my revived princess.
Come to me, my love, and we'll coo like
morning doves.

GEL:
Uh, Dad—

BOY:
That's not a real person. Nosterafu kung fu.

KICK:
I know what I am doing, Boy. Here's the
passel of souls you wanted, Doc. Ready to be reamed.

KICKING ANTELOUPE HANDS OVER A REAM OF PAPERS.

MAD MAN:
Great. But this resurrection didn't go
as planned. The girl can't talk, right.

BUFF MAIDEN:
Murph phole kichi maambo. Eek, eek, eek.
Wooooik!

BUFFALO MAIDEN ZOMBIE DOUBLE STARTS DIVING AND RESURFACING, WITH FISH, THEN STARTS SWIMMING OUT INTO THE HORIZON, WHERE A WOLF IS HEADED.

KICK:
Here's your damned soul dispossession forms.

MAD MAN:
Well some good will come of my experiments.

KICK:
After her! Turn this dingy around before
she's exhausted. She'll undergo the
Second Death and be lost in limbo forever.

GEL:
Oh great. Another wild goose chase.

BOY:
What's that noise?
LOUD WHISTLING NOISE LIKE A BOMB ARRIVING.
A SATELLITE AFIRE FALLS TO EARTH AND NAILS
BUFFALO MAIDEN THE ZOMBIE.
WOLF CIRCLES AROUND CONFUSED AND
DISORIENTED.

MAN:
Are there any sandwiches left over?
Cheese cake? I'm starved. I forgot
just how many fingers it took to make
the sound of one hand clapping. Maybe
I went overboard, huh? Hey, is that
devil's fork lit up using Atlantis's

crystal? Neat! Are you trying out for the
job of Alien Messiah, dude? If so I'm
so very glad that I quit the Hari Krishnas.
I smell double devil chocolate cake. Come
on now, give. Thank you. Thank you, girl.

GEL:
De nada, Boddhevista.

TIM:
The cracker barrel kracken.

KICK:
Oh damn. All that work for naught.
And why would I try to be an Alien
Messiah when I have microbes and E-coli
to herd and pimples to farm?

GABBY:
Uh--I don't know--to become a hero sandwich;
a beam in God's idol during the Dark Days
of our Doomsday Apocalypse Luncheon on
a sabbath soiree.

MEATBALL:
To feed your wet dog ego. I guess.

KICK:
Alright. My free energy will power your
floating castles. Don't just sit there
wallowing. Plug into my trident.

GABBY:
Riiight. Fix up my Venus shaver.
Muffy Cleaver has five o'clock shadow.

GEL:
Here, borrey my electric eel. It will
laminate your menu, doll.

GEL HOLDS UP AN ELECTRIC EEL THAT SMOKES AND SPARKS.

BOY:
And if you require a drier clime
hop any passing mossy back toy-tuss.
Next week you can return the favor and
hand out kisses. I'm all yours; sabes?

GABBY:
Yuck. You're sick.

BOY:
Here. Take it.

BOY HOLDS OUT HAND. GABBY TAKES IT. SHE'S SHOCKED.

GABBY:
Ow! That stunt just bounced you out
of the submarine races, Wolfgang.

BOY:
Free energy for the blind and lost
puppies.

REENTER SINGER AND SALLY.

GUIT:
I sing a tune to Great Neptune who
charges all my batteries. I tried
to give a penny a volt but he don't
want no salary. Now we live on New
Atlantis, the sea around our skirts.
I would give him the skin off my back
but--see!--we have lost our shirts.

SALLY:
Neptune's symbol is fracture. All it
does is clash.

GABBY:
I don't trust the weeping bastard
for giving us this bath.

TIM:
Where are those lousy scientists?
I've had enough paddling from these
Markee De Sad. I feel like I'm
channeling to host a toast of crab.

BOY:
Someone man the keyboards;
another of you play bass.

SALLY:
After this land-sea divorce, Ma culls
the human race.

BOAT BROADCASTING NEWS OVER LOUD SPEAKER PASSES BY.

CNN:
The West Coast has fallen; the East Coast has been swamped Maine to Florida. A swath of states in the Midwest the Dakotas to West Texas have sunk into a giant sinkhole. The United States is now the Divided States! The Rockies on the west side; the Appalachians on the east side; the Midwest gone to picnic with Hades as a blanket. A huge hole has swallowed Ohio and the surrounding states.

KICK:
Yep, Hades, Pluto, my lil' bro. Gotta love that boy. Doesn't scare, no fear in a hair or toenail. Calls'em like he sees'em. Takes Persephone on a six month hayride. Ya-huh.

ENTER ZODIACS WITH SCIENTISTS.

CNN:
A new island has arisen in the Bermuda Triangle. Who knows where the equator or the poles are? Calls us if you discover.

KICK:
Two more days of this trial-by-shark and tsunami. Then those who survive the aftermath will be safe.

SCI ONE:
Aftermath! What kind of numbers are we talking here?

BOY:
Don't get yer dingy in a sling. Tell us, Aquaman.

KICK:
We have bodies to bury and houses to replace.
Decades of digging, centuries to change.

GEL:
Waste recycling centers to incorporate.
Nuclear sludge to bury. Someplace.

GABBY:
Coal plants to dry out or rebuild. Maybe
tap the lava rising from Tolken's mirage.

TIM:
The Ring of Power shall be mine when
light comes lancing up my spine. We've
made a promise to joust with the Divine.
To hand over our paper routes and our Keds.

MEATBALL:
Take out an ad to praise the Ultimate
Climate Regulator, Land Reformer, and
Lemonade Stand.

TIM:
I don't mind acknowledging a smart Lord
of the castle if I have a place to fort up,

when the zombies learn to swim and the mud freezes.
SCI ONE:
Oh you poor children, God is dead.
Washington drowned.

GABBY:
Can you pay up before your promise expires?

SCI TWO:
We're good for every dime. Line up. Line up.

SCIENTISTS PAY KIDS. THEN THEY RAISE THEIR PADDLES.

SCI TWO:
What's this?

KICK:
Cash is worthless, kiddos. Fort Knox is
a shipwreck. But I know where to get a
good used Chinese sub. And GPS points.

GABBY:
Twenty one gun salute.

TIM:
Whack-a-mole', affectionados.

KIDS DRIVE OFF SCIENTISTS. THEIR ZODIACS DEFLATE. THE SCIENTISTS SWIM OFF HOLDING ONTO BUOYS.

MEATBALL:
So much for your daily horoscope.

TIM:
Well, spill it. Status report.

MEATBALL:
I found the mountain. Let off the
lady and ole man. Came back with blisters.

SPUD:
The compass kept spinning after a couple
hours. Now North is East, South is West,
sunrise is wherever it is whenever it
decides to stop this hula.
KENNY:
The arrow points towards the Rock House.
The feathers tickle the ocean and Hawaii.
I'm so hungry but you can't eat money.
Let's go diving for fishing gear at the
Bait Shop.

MEATBALL:
How'd we do dat?

KENNY:
We'll mark the spot with our new improved
NEW AGE GPS. It's all the hunting dog
you'll ever need, Elvis.

MEATBALL:
Damn it. Where's mine? Not fair.
Life is screwy.

KICK:
Here. I have an extra.

MEATBALL:
I got hung up on the nipples of Neptune.
I went diving for coral sea weed cake.
I scryed the runes and tattoos of the
colossus drowning in the lagoon.

GABBY:
Someone show me how to read the starfish.
How to gump the bumps in this meteoroid.

GABBY HOLDS UP A METEORITE ONTO WHICH A STARFISH IS ATTACHED.

TIM:
Come with me through a swamp of garbage
and we'll eat MRE's with Hope and Joy.

SPUD:
Love is finding and claiming a submerged
stash of Hostess and Mars Bars.

LIL BIT:
Tomorrow we'll mosh and gorge with
abandonment, playing tag on a barge.
KENNY:
We'll make stringers of corpses to inter;
Great Spirit give us the courage to not hurl.

QUEENY:
I got my eye on a yacht down in Tampa
because Hyannis Port is no longer there.

RALPH:
Someone borrey me a curry comb please
for the rampant needles in my hairdo.

ALL KIDS:
We are the brats of the Aquaprofit;
No one is giving us a chance. We're hardly warm but spoiled rotten so let RIPA do his dance. Under the waves lie the brash and brave who couldn't get outta the way of--Oops. No one gave us a float or life saver--Don't be shooting us those dirty looks! Begone, sea turtles!

KICK:
Ah, my feisty star fish baptized by blood and rising above the flood, to tell this story forever and a day, to grandkids. Babe, here's to you. (kiss, kiss, wave)

SINGER AND SALLY:
Fiddle, Nero, for your breakfast. Rome's had its day.

GEL:
Now, Glory, where will we crash.

FINIS

DOOMSDAY'S DONUTS TWO

EXTERIOR: A DOCKYARD WHERE A CROWD OF BOATERS ARE EMBARKING ON A JOURNEY WHILE SURROUNDED BY OTHERS WHO ARE ASSISTING AND HINDERING THEIR ACTIVITIES. THERE ARE MOUNTEBANKS, SINGERS, VENDORS, GOVERNMENT OFFICIALS, AND THE ASSORTED PICKPOCKET AND CON MAN. ON A SOAPBOX STANDS A BLACK LADY PREACHER PREACHING AND CARRYING ON.

LADY SPIRITUALIST:
I'm going to the graveyard to soak up the divine light:
Climbing Boot Hill just to see the sights.
I'm not frightened: I hope to behold the light shining
through the caskets in a blaze of afterlife. I'm
traveling to the boneyard to breathe the celestial
airs; watch the angels cavorting up and down the
stairs. To witness death's maudlin kiss because life
isn't fair. Smooching with the Devil whose dance
is debonair. Someone blast that trumpet touching
Gabriel's lips; blow smoke into the clouds to give
our blues a lift. If you see St Peter's robes
furrowing the drifts of the seventh sphere, you've
received the gift of grace. Judgment Day is coming,
Judgment Day is coming. So move your carcass on over.
Judgment Day is near. Now welcome your soul's new
hover board. We are on the verge; we are so daring.
Now Virgil and Darrell, get your rears in gear. No fear!

VENDOR:

Bring your fish for the fish fry. Cutlets for the barbecue. Taters for the spud salad. And your baggage for the stew. A New Age is forming. A New Age is here. Come on down, you rats and roaches of the Apocalypse. Forge your sins and trials at the fa'ar, you New Age Vulcans. Run down the pedestrian whiners. All you pilots, jump into your fliers. All the mechanics, crunch your pliers. All the housewives, tango with your driers. All the renegades, shout your defiance! Corpus Christi, here we are.

HOBO:

Fish fry in the sky. Fish fry in the sky. Open up your eyes to your gifts divine.

LADY SPIRIT (tossing Hobo a quarter)

A new day comes to bounce this twilight. In the cemetary the pine boards are alight. Burning like the Parvo lighthouse. All you mortals cry, all cadavers pout, for the new day takes no prisoners no how. 'Cause the belly of the Beast is stinky; throw off your shackles 'n' gizmos. Shed your stones and chips in favor of immortality. Yessiree bob!

VENDOR:

On your toes from tulipping to the boneyard--
You won't need no credit--the Word excuses fraud--
your breath will be so fetid it'll curdle Magog.

HOBO:

Fish fry in the sky. Fish fry in the sky. Open up, hush puppies, to ketsup divine.

PROPHET IN HAIR SHIRT:
Come to me and we'll be free; swim to islands in an azure sea. Follow the sun and meet the One—

ENTER BOY WITH DUFFLE BAG.

BOY:
The sun ain't shining, bozo.

PROPHET:
--who gives us immortality. Children are the masters of our lives—

BOY:
Except, unless they're bastards. Recalculate! Instead of a karmic whip, a lucky blip follows an unfortunate slip.

PROPHET:
--we serve the leaders of manana—

BOY:
Banana splits extra nuts.

PROPHET:
--in them God and in them love to balance the world's karma.

BOY:
But who will push start my Karman Ghia?

HOBO:
I live in a box, I eat out a can, hide from
the rain, run from the man. When the devil
tries to getcha: run, river, run. When the
supper bell rings: run, river, run. When
the hammer's 'bout to hit: run, river, run.
When the tsunami foos yer kung: run, river, run.

CHEVY COMES UP AND GIVES HOBO A HOSTESS CUP CAKE. HE SEES KRISSY AND CAT WAITING. SPEAKS TO THE AIR BETWEEN THEM.

CHEVY:
Lose the shoes, kick it to the river, toss red
wrigglers into the eddies; above where the mud
cat makes her nest.

KRISSY:
He's sniffed you out, Cat. Listen for next clue.

CHEVY:
Ask the delta nymph to aid our searching.

CAT & KRISSY:
That's you. Oooough. (pointing at each other)

GOVERNMENT LADY WITH CLIPBOARD AND PEN SURVEYS THE CROWD AND OCEAN.

GOV.COM:
I wanna be a FEMA frauline and tent millions on the
prairie. Bring man and mosquito together with
clouds of nasty weather. Give everyone blankets
and a goat, trade MRE's for a hungry joke. Move

in, come on over to FEMA Town. Fine scenery,
loving cows. Erase your hunger and them frowns.
Wanna be a FEMA frauline. Treat with FEMA sleepers.

MEATBALL:
Here's another rubber stamper for the Golden
Boy. He sold his soul to rule the world.
Sold his future to gain the vote. Sold his former
wife to marry into the KGB, who now blindly wears
his stinking Nazi sneakers. Sold his member
to the boneyard to pork Lady Liberty. Then
slapped his ass on the face of Congress to
hear'em squeal.

ENTER KICKING ANTELOUPE WITH HIS TWINS, GEL
AND BOY, BAGS OF CLOTHES.

KICK:
The stars beam knowledge at our bodies, but
it is up to us to do our own laundry. A woman
was born to love. A baby to cry. And a man
was born to dine. A sword is made to cleave
and shape. Our keen souls, tempered in this
oven of clay--one day to shed its gloss,
en fin to fly. The stars and not the galaxy,
the cream and not the dugs, the reflection and
not the silver, the moth and not the flamingo,
the ruby and not the slippers. The gaucho and
the thunder racing the hides. Aztec maiden
weeping to be defiled. Princess more peaked
than Chloe in her abandon, evacuating the
Nothingness to be herself Great Void.

ENTER PINCHE PENNY, A NEWCOMER TO THE OUTFIT,
WHO DRAGS A SUITCASE ALONG THE DOCK. SHE LOOKS AT FLOATILLA OF
RAFTS AND JON BOATS AND CANOES. OTHER KIDS ALSO GATHER TO BOARD.

PENNY:
Permission to come aboard with my emory.

GEL:
So, why should we bring you along? Eh?

PENNY:
Miz Miza, my boss, has a ton of Kuggerands.
Three suitcases full. Arr arr arr, mates.

BOY:
Sweet. Works for me.

MEATBALL:
There's something fungible about being solvent.
Right, Miss Creosote Flower?
GEL:
Oh yeah. Unless yo have to swim laps, crawler.

MEATBALL:
Like apples and oranges—

MEATBALL GRABS GEL.

GEL:
What! I ain't bobbing, Fred, in your Fruit-of
the-Looms.

MEATBALL:
Let me peel your Granny Smiths. Make apple
sauce. Hup, too green and skinny.

MEATBALL LETS GO OF GEL'S SUSPENDERS. GEL FALLS.

MEATBALL:
Let me squeeze your navel oranges, I'll turn
you into OJ.

MEATBALL HOVERS OVER PENNY.

MEATBALL:
Can I kiss your grapes before Chardonay
betrays us? Grab a chocolate eclair, yeah—

PENNY:
Dude, hands off the lamb chops. Gah. Look
but not mango, chutney. Yuck. Sanitation!
I am not an artic fox nor am I a vole you
want to know. In the barnyard too many cocks,
north or south a wobbling pole. If I go out
to water the grass there's a woodpecker on
my ass! When I'm strolling through the back
yard, I get hailed by a passing hot rod.
Everywhere you shake a stick, you will wallop
some gnarly dick. Take your pick of dim pool
halls, they're filled with knocking balls.
One way to put a stop to this? Make the
prick your bitch. Your bitch! Your bitch!
Then bewitch him with a twist. If he cries,
slap the dick and lend him to some other bitch.

MEATBALL:
Does this mean you're available?

PENNY:
Don't try wading in this tidal pool because it creeks Let no trout pass, especially those sportsmen who think they can plunge in, roll out, no consequence. Therefore your ecology is demonology. Hell I bet your ugly stick still has yo moma's mud all over it. Please, Chad, keep your lure lowered and your kinky lines to yourself. Don't wonder why Molly coddles the dimpled worm of rank desire, jes' keep dem Valentines posted at the fence line.

GEL:
Yeah, Dude. No boundaries. Big slobber, no tissue. Did anyone take his distemper this morning? God's bollocks. Jesus sneezes. Dub a Bubba an' hump till you holla, trollop trawler. Back.

BOY:
We can no more contain our hobgloblins than we can leach the saline from our jeans.
PENNY:
It'd be easier to reduce the Rockies to a rock pile.

MEATBALL:
I agree. It's easier to curtail a dog's caboose after lunch than it is to ask a kid to act right. You know that. I know that. Uh... Um. Gas break. Phew!

GEL:
Hold that propane, Wilbur. Gag.

CHEVY:
Come on and grab your sinkers; a golden hook would be alright. We will cut new cane poles in the ripe sunlight.

CHEVY POSES IN FRONT OF KRISSY AND CAT.

TIM:
Don't try to understand, just delve into her jodpurs. Stop fighting the emotion, slide through white waters.

EVERYONE BUT MEATBALL MOVES ON.

MEATBALL:
Pause your dogs, Honey. I am aching for bisquotti; let us measure our bliss by thimblesfull and avoid barracuda schools. Dog paddle past jelly fish and octopus for they love to sting and crush. Some golden chains and silver cages weigh our days and foul our pages. Each of us holds the weight of Eternity's spinning lure and porpoise of the Infinite. Squeak, eek! Ploink!

ENTER MR MIZA AN OLD MAN HOLDING AN UMBRELLA.

MEL:
Howdy.

MEATBALL:
Auf weener stern, Von Munchengruber.

MEL:
Gazundheit. Here. Cough drop. Cherry flavor.

MEATBALL:
Danke, Danube.

MEL:
How'd you know my pop's name is Danil? Are you a psychic Hoyle?

MEATBALL:
Lufa.

MEL:
Nice to meetcha, Red Baron. Grab that bag.

REENTER PINCHE PENNY. MEATBALL TAKES UP ONE BAG.

PENNY:
Don't let this laugh-riot give you genital warts. Whatever he has, it's catching.

MEATBALL:
We're not that way at all—

PENNY:
Goot.

MEL:
Are my bags loaded? Is my coin
collection in good order?

PENNY:
Yeah. Yeah. Da.

MEATBALL:
Sal urine now.

MEATBALL DROPS BAG ON PENNY'S FOOT.

PENNY:
Put a rock in it, Crackhead. Blast my
ass to the Everglades. Feed me to the
gators and boa. Tickle my snares with
silk nylons. Done?

MEATBALL:
San Antonio! Where's the cutoff valve,
Manuela?

PENNY:
Oh go sing your anthem to the seashore
during slime ball season.

MEATBALL:
Here, let me grease that knothole in
your boxers with some loogie tunes.
And my balls go jingle jangle jingo.

PENNY:
Att! Silence in the peanut section. Hut!

REENTER OTHER YOUNGSTERS. TIM AND KRISSY,
CHEVY AND CAT MOVE FORWARD.

TIM:

Cover your red ears fuming in the wild.

GEL:

If you wanna play zoom zoom, grab some
broom straw, boss.

KRISSY:

If you wanna find Xanadu, hum on your
own rusty kazoo.

DENNY:

If you gotta crush on Lulu, practice your
sobs on a voodoo doll.

KRISSY

If you think she's foo foo, then you're
cuckoo, darlin'.

GEL:

Let's make a mess of goo goo and spin
that poopoo platter, la.

MEATBALL:

This pancake can't cook soon enough for me.

DENNY:

Crepes Suzette, raspberry on the side.

KRISSY:

Crepes Suzette, bacon you can bite.

TIM:
Lioness canines pierce your screaming Sahara.
Moonlit melody. And if you live to see the
dawn, tears like dew on your awning wash away
your innocence in the thimble of her pirate bootie.

GEL:
Bring me to the isle. Ship me cross the
waves. Serve me up with salad unto my
dying fade!

MEATBALL:
I'll see you in my crystal ball.

GEL:
Vamos a Corpus Christi, y'all. Ondalay!

MEL:
I've been digging a hole in the mountain.
I've been breaking down rock for gold.
Making a tunnel deep in the earth's bowels;
asking Mother Nature to enrich my holdings.
I been diggin' diggin' diggin' in the mountain.
I been breakin' breakin' breakin' the bedrock.
Tunnelin' tunnelin' tunnelin' like a gopher.
Hopin' hopin' hopin' for a fountain of gold.

EXIT PENNY WITH SUITCASE FOLLOWING MR MEL MIZA.

MEATBALL:
There's no past or future--they's only
bootay. There are no great books, only
great bazookas. If I had a penny for

every time I thought of sushi I'd buy
the Taj Mahal twicet for my lovely.
And my balls go jingle, jangle, jingo.

GEL:
There's a flea in my pants makes me
wanna dance. There's an itch in my shorts
scratchin' paradise. There's a shimmy
in my chimney burning the house down.
There's a sty in my eye makes me wink
and rowl like a holy cowgirl. Don't let
my kitty maul your yogurt yurt.

DENNY:
Iron filings heat up our blood destroying
our hearts with foiled love.

KRISSY:
Observe the love bugs coupling like
Cupids in the air. The cats and rats
of the underpier frolic in their furry
fury. Sex rules the fish, fowl, fauna,
and females.

DENNY:
So?
KRISSY:
I'm so glad it bothers me not. I'm immune.
(sighs)

DENNY:
Just wait, Gorgon. Your cut will out too.
Then you'll play for Ouches and Boo Hoo's.

TIM:
For you will wonder and scratch your head
with charcoal and look for another vixen
to overhaul your scabby trousers.

CAT (to Krissy):
Ask 'im. Whatcha wan me to doogle--lick
your boots, wrangler?

CHEVY (to Krissy):
I got blown in from the sky. My star is
Obi Mobi 117. I wonder often if I am a
guy drug inside another girl's barbecue
wagon.

KRISSY:
The melodrama. I know. Slap hands and
tonsils, blow me up to a dirigible.

CHEVY:
We don't know why we've come so far
propagating that great wild distance
from afar. Freckled by the cosmic sneeze
and geometry that grids thought as we scream.
Ever falling in our dream.

KRISSY:
Every star calling like a beacon to guide
the bow of every seeker. Every person has
heart so soft—

CHEVY:
That it should get mussel topped. Here's
a beanie.

CHEVY GIVES KRISSY HIS WOOLEN CAP.

KRISSY:
Danke.

CHEVY:
The diamond inside my third eye, that rules
the mad dog, may be fractured.

KRISSY:
Stroke it, stroke it.

CHEVY:
Stop.
I got rattle snake bones in this vest. To kill off sharks or pests.

KRISSY GRABS AND HUGS CHEVY SPONTANEOUSLY.

CHEVY:
I can't breathe. I can, I can breathe. If I
was named Jack would you be my golden goose?

KRISSY:
Avacado, avacado, guava, habenero.

CHEVY:
Odelay! You have a way, with me.

KRISSY:
Hooga boogah!

CHEVY:
In this hand I hold the breast of Time, that

spiral sublimiinoble. The stutter stomping
miracle that masquerades the imbecile. Shut!
This isle of abundance holding Circe's cereal.
Up! The water mystery barnacle that pierces
love's spherical. T---T---Those tangential
flowers that empower the masculine, the warrior
principle. WWWe chose you and smooze truly
wonderful. Around us are those amp blessed
imp shed a kiss of the unutterable mandible.

CAT TRIES TO DRAG KRISSY AWAY BUT KRISSY IS OBJURATE,STAYING.

CHEVY:

In this hand All-metta finger of Goll the
spider toothed ecstasy that webs fraility,
the cauldron emspiced recipe trinity wised
as a baby. As my eyes fail me I worship your
deeper energy e quality wave ravening as musical.
I do the math backwards leaching onto her clavicle.
The barrow earth pip seeking aurial conspiracy.
Tree mending us salt vands of fish hook. The
thighbone of paradise feeding all desire paradox.
Mammary munching entree' and register at the
doorway; guardian strangler triangle that geomates
with strawberry. Pepper mangled angel delivering
pizza rebelry. HHHit takes the soul away awhile
to reap her mystery.

CAT SLAPS CHEVY AND DRAGS KRISSY AWAY FROM HIM.

ALL THE YOUNGSTERS SING AND PLAY WHAT INSTRUMENTS ARE HANDY. MEATBALL WITH GUITAR DOES BOB DYLAN.

ALL KIDS:
I was searching for Nirvana on the shores
of the Abyss when I drowned within the
vortex, choking on my bliss. I tried to
fight my demon, inhaled St Helen's fire;
burnt my hands getting greedy and called
Destiny a liar. I froze on the tundra
chasing Big Foot into the mists; pulled
honey from gold creek and gave my Fate a kiss.
I howled like that blizzard when it swept
my soul away--cried to the angels asking
the Great Spirit to behave. I'm too high
to be flyin'; at the limit of my strength.
A horse shoe thrown my Orion a-followin'
my bent. A horse shoe thrown by Orion—

GEL:
The footility of fixing Atlas's arches.
There's a sparkle in Zeus's eyeball and
it takes my breath away. I want to
strangle in his dreadlocks and hear
Cerebus bay. The marching of dead souls
keeps me awake most nights; who will oppose
them when the daylight reveals their weary
sighs?

PENNY:
A ghoul possessed my pillow and licked
my ear lobe raw. All that I can say is:
Begone but not till dawn.

GABBY:
People notice my loose tongue and tell

me off, oh yeah. But I have an itinerary that maps the meandering ode to Paris's Rue de Snail. Yum.

PENNY:
The groove is beneath the waves but we've lost the scuba tech.

GEL:
Someone help me raise Davy Jones' locket from this pirate wreck.

ALL KIDS:
You're not so mighty after all. You're not so mighty once you fall. Let's leave the might to mountains tall and heave the boulders like beach balls. You're not so mighty after all.

GEL:
You're not so mighty as you bail. Let's leave the might to fishing tales and hooking up with Jonah's whale.

ALL KIDS:
You're not so mighty after all. Let's leave the might to baby's breath and grinding corpses into wealth.

JEFF:
Look around you. We're in a perfect world. There's no bankers.

MEL:
So, Dr. Mengele, what am I? Chopped liver?

JEFF:
Are you sure you're a Hebe? Show
us your gold.
MEL:
I got this tattoo at the Berlin games:
#69FUSOB88. It cost me two tons of gold coin.
And eighty eight pounds of buttah.

BOY:
I see it! It's bonafide. Velcro,
Moses. You ripped it.

CAT:
Why is this happening? And why must
we endure?
KRISSY:
You sinned and now you must atone.

CHEVY:
What tone? C-sharp? B-flat? Angel
choir, drop the bridge.

KRISSY:
What do you know?

CHEVY:
I can fiddle your Strativarious
in various frets at midnight.
Work your clef over the cliff.
And avalanche.

KRISSY:
You see too far into the future, wood-eye.

ALL KIDS:
When reviewing the past all we dream's
chopped liver. When the corn don't
last, we'll eat chopped liver. When
the cat's got our tongue, we'll speak
chopped liver. When we're mad at the
world, we'll spank chopped liver. When
we want wisdom, we'll smoke chopped liver.
And when the sun don't shine, we'll
poop chopped liver.

PENNY:
Beats brains and montain oysters.

MEL:
I tell you guys. I've seen the world.
Sure they gave me gratis this tattoo
the mark of Hades; but I've endured
` the hate and got the girl. Now I'm
old and rich trying to survive, this
flood. You know my mojo. I don't
wanna die. Do not honk for me for I
am dust. When everything gets dusty,
everybody's grunge.

MEATBALL:
And my balls go jingle, jangle, jingo.

ENTER GOVERNMENT SOCIAL WORKER.

GOV.COM:
Alright, alright, alright. Line up,
you losers. Line up for your checks.
If you outta line you go broke. Keep
your hands in plain sight right. Line
up for checks.

MEL:
Mel Miza, I'm expecting.

GOV.COM:
Yep. Mel Miza, according to the Death
Master File, which is never wrong, you
are deceased. Is that really you in
that ID? How'd you burn your fingertips?
Don't do no more acid. Hippies. Next!

MEL:
This seems like a revolving door I'm
stuck in. Pinche Penny, has all my
luggage arrived?

PENNY:
So loaded we're ready to fire the ordinance,
Cappy. What's the name of our boat?

MEL:
Alma's Dark Night.

PENNY:
On my soul, a heavy wench. El Loco Noche.

GABBY:
So dark it reeks of shocko mousse.

GABBY AND MEL MOVE ON. MEATBALL HOVERS. PENNY PULLS ON SUITCASE, THEN LETS IT DOWN AGAIN.

PENNY:

I want to steer your fragile tugs as the
New Age starts. Life is easy but fate
is hard. Cruise on down my boulevard.
The old world passes before our eyes
following the death of Time. A new world
comes from ice and mud, miracles and
tainted blood. We must move past the
wandering poles, toes frozen by the cold.
Move our homes to suspect shores, past
an army of alien spores. As a comet
speeds 'tween Earth and Mars, come and
checker my Ouija board.

MEATBALL:

You want to blame someone, you need heroes
to kill. You hope the torture ends It
surely can't be real. We are being tested
over and over again. Let me jump into
your gull-winged ess elle, Mercedes. Help
my balls go jingle, jangle, jingo.

PENNY:

Ah you pup. Go away! Here's an eagle.
Go buy a clue. That's the rub, my
Beauregard. (aside) Row me home 'tween
those salty arms, Mr Beaujango.

KIDS MINGLE. HAIR-SHIRTED PROPHET DANCING, WEARING SWAN LIVESAVER AND FLOATIES.

PROPHET:
Gather near. Follow me to Shangrila. All your wishes will come true in the sands of Malibu. You are the chosen ones with moony eyes and eager tongues. Travel with me: off into the waves of Eternity. Throw off the shackles and get ready to tackle Godhead. Follow me to Shangrila, come meet Mr Buddha in Elysian Fields. No big deal. No problema, mi paloma. Take a bite of karma, come home.

SALES GIRL:
Coats. Thick wool socks. Thermal blankets. Heavens, it gonna be cold. Don't swallow the fruit salad. Get ready! Parkas. Ski pants. Snow boots. Fur hats. Ear muffs. Long johns. Down undies. Don't be caught in gym shorts when Mr Freeze slaps your toes with a hash tag and a behoffawatamus bites your Michael Kors off.

GOV.COM:
Okay okay. Make yer choice. WC Fields or money. Free money from yer loving Uncle Sam. If you gramps can't make it, bring in their ID. And if they're not on the Master Death List, you're golden. Line up for your check. Free money from your Republican well-wishers. Vote Republican and stop Doomsday at the Wall.

REENTER PENNY WITH BAGS UNDER HER EYES.

PENNY:
I'm so tired I can barely roll.

ENTER GEL AND GABBY.

PENNY:
That Gonzo is hideous. Is he a fag?
Because it behooves me to chase centaurs
with diamonds in their clop.

PENNY STAMPS FOOT.

GEL:
He yanks my chain.

GABBY:
The drain hole's fulla goo.

PENNY:
We should sabotage him. He's a rotten egg.

GEL:
How? He has a Fart Knoxious force-field.

PENNY:
There are ways, believe me. That
creep-a-zoid is going down, but not on me.

THE THREE GIRLS GIGGLE AS THEY EXIT. BOY AND
TIM FOLLOW THEM THEN STOP.

TIM:
Did you catch that? Nefarious as a mullet
grabbing for your wallet.

BOY:
Naw. But I got something on my geiger
counter: six, seven, beep.

HIS PHONE BEEPS. EXIT TWO GUYS. ENTER MEL MIZA AND KRISSY AND CAT.

MEL:
So tell me, what do you use for cash?

KRISSY:
Socks, bumps, or strokes. Back rubs,
you know.

KRISSY PUTS HER FINGER IN HER MOUTH AND POPS HER CHEEK.

MEL:
Really. What about coin?

CAT:
There ain't no paper worth the wipe.
The government's dick is comatose, Jack.

MEL:
Well. What would you do for this gold
necklace?

KRISSY:
I'd be your lily frog legs.

CAT:
No! For an hour. You trampoline.

MEL:
Gosh.

KRISSY:
Here. Pretty.

MEL:
No. It doesn't match me. Keep it.

KRISSY:
Wow. You're like Mr. Impossible.

CAT:
This scent is of dingleberry, grizzlie.
I don't go out with anybody over filthy.

MEL:
This ring is too small for me. Look.
Ruby. Betcha it fits ya.

CAT:
Neat! Wowsah. I'm your girl Friday, Mack.

KRISSY:
The mustard in a tub of turkey.

MEL:
Alright. I get it. Help me move my
luggage over just a little.

KRISSY:
Why do you carry your bags wherever you
hang, mister?

MEL:
I'm superstitious about my old photos.
My childhood collection of encyclopedia.
Attached you might say.

CAT:
Oh.

EXIT MEL, BAGS, AND TWO GIRLS. ENTER KICKING ANTELOUPE AND CHEVY.

KICK:
This Mida is kinda spooky. Tail him.
See if he has any heads in his carpetbag.

CHEVY:
Louis Vuitton. What do I get in return? Huh?

KICK:
Uh, foot massage by lobsters and anemone.
Man o' war. Sea razortail, crab, the
spiked whip of rays 'n' catfish cow licks.

CHEVY:
I'm gone.

EXIT CHEVY.

KICK:
Nothing encourages a lad like vipers.

ENTER MEATBALL IN CAT HALLOWEEN COSTUME.

MEATBALL:
There you are. Tell me, since you are so wise and wheazy, what does a guy do to improve his princess, er, princesses plural?

KICK:
Well, don't let the moss grow on the sunny side of your harpoon. Raise that petard! Keep your whistle sharp and your powder dry. You don't obtain water nymphs and dryads unless you can enchant and ensorcel them with honeyed flies and buzzing promises. To dig the mine you gotta seed the way with gold. The weakest time of the day is before the chamberpot fills. So plan around that. Keep your head down and your chin up. If you need to practice do some push-ups, guy. Don't just make squares in burgers and slap on the cheese.

MEATBALL:
Chamber pot?! Weakest days are right after the--you know. Rabbit season. Which one should I—

KICK:
She has butter in her fly, a bite to her licorice, stars in her eyes and strawberries in her hair. She's got a frog in her lip, fire in her fingertips; juice in her goggles, and a donkey in her kick. She has a black hole in her heart, a tiger in her bite, the Infinity Man has lost, and Eternity in her smile. What? If I knew her name I wouldn't need my

own. I could shine like the dawn and never
feel old.

MEATBALL:
Thanks, pops. The voyage. Whirlpool. Kracken,
got it. Bye. And my balls...

EXIT MEATBALL.

KICK:
It takes a shipwreck or two to cotton onto--
Hut. Time to get going--her drift.

CANOES WITH KIDS MOVE ALONG, KICKING ANTELOUPE ON A RAFT WITH GEL AND BOY PADDLING.
PENNY AND MEL ON RAFT TOO.

TIM:
I'm cold and I'm shriveled up as a prune.
My grapes have withered into fignoramuses.

JEFF:
My GPS is out-of-order as is my Timex.

GEL:
All the earth satellites will be going for
a dive as the planet's spin stops completely.

GABBY:
Oh what do you know?
GEL:
Aren't you feeling heavy, gorda?

GABBY:
Uh, it's just the, sangfroid lemur. Isn't it?

GET:
It ain't that no-fly zone being activated.
When there's less spin they less centrifugal
force, less lessening of our weight. We gain
twenty pounds instantly.

TIM:
But I'm feeling light headed, dandelion.

MEATBALL:
That's the sea sickness of being on DART.
Rapid transit. And being on this raft.
Raft surely.

TIM:
Rapture, idiot. Rap---

ENTER OLE WOMAN AND OLE MAN IN TUB.

OLE WOMAN:
Oh Christ, it's the End Days.

OLE MAN:
Now, Darling.

OLE WOMAN:
I can feel it in my ass.

CHEVY:
Don't the owl paddling this washtub know,
this kitty's mad?

KICK:
Some feel light headed as their body's
weight increases. Some are caught up
in inertia as the slag thickens.

OLE WOMAN:
Take that back, I'm not a slag. Nor fat.
Big mouth bass in a gloomy bayou.
OLE MAN:
Sir! Sir! They know nothing at all.

OLE WOMAN:
Where will you mark it, Mr Byrd?
What place did you place the North Pole and Santa?
Give it to us. We trust your word, your word!
Where'll Sonnie rest if there's no clue to due West?
Does the moon rise over here, or over there?
Where does it lie, Mr Byrd? Mr Byrd!
Where in the world is the pivot?
We dig and we dig, churning with the herd.
Way too soiled by the divots.
Is the moon at her breast or her thighs--Fine!
The woman of the mountain so described
Points the way the rythmn stays.
Where did it go, Mr Byrd? Mr Byrd!
Where's the canary in the mine;
Common knowledge is denied.
it's fallen "off its perch"? That's absurd.
Absurd as a songbird reciting Psalms in rythme.
Oh where did the canary go, Mr Byrd?
It's all at variance with the science of the times.
We have a right to know! Who'll tell Santa?
Oh my head, you're so dead, Mr Byrd. Mr Byrd!

OLE WOMAN THRASHES THE TWO TUBBIES AWAY.

GABBY:
Speaking of big goose, where's this submarine
you were bragging about? Heh?

GEL:
Yeah, Dad.

BOY:
Old Mariner, you wanna go trollin'?

KICK:
Now now. Behave. I'm screwy as a
Phillips highball right now. Seeing stars.

AWKWARD PAUSE.

MEATBALL:
I'm thirsty. Where in the world are
we gonna find clean water?

ALL KIDS:
Watta watta watta, where have yous gone?
Sweaty watta bottle, listen to my storm.

GABBY:
Potable watta. (motions to her groin)
Now available. Save me from a quick dip.
And trade one exposure from the colder.

TIM LEADING OTHERS:
Oh hell no!

KICK:
Survival of the fittest, grab ahold.
Who's thirsty? Pucker up, suckers.

GABBY:
You first, Meatball. You look a bit
peckish in that mouse trap.

MEATBALL:
Ladies first, lead the way, Mon Derrierre.

GEL:
Since when? Death Valley?

TIM:
There's little food so I'm going on
a juice fast.

GEL:
Not so fast, meteor.

GABBY:
Yeah, porky. Are you hiding and hoarding?

GEL:
Shame.

TIM:
You're not the hippopotomi, sweet cheeks.
Besides I ate so much I'm going off to
the last boat, start Rhode Island. Care
to compare?

ALL KIDS:
Ew! You stinker! Bomb's aweigh, Dr Strangelove.

REENTER OLE WOMAN AND OLE MAN.

OLE WOMAN:
Sir! Sir! I'm not a slag. I'm a lager.

OLE MAN:
I may spawn ripples of rapture in her bathroom, but I'll never fathom the sphinx.

OLE WOMAN:
Why is that young man mooning me?

OLE MAN:
I gather he's making a chipmunk prediction. You'll see, Diana.

OLE WOMAN:
His wise crack over the waters reminds me of our honeymoon.

OLE MAN:
Poison oak for tissue. We scratched our libidos for weeks. What I wouldn't give---
Oh la la.

OLE WOMAN AND OLE MAN FLOAT AWAY. MEL AND PENNY TOGETHER.

MEL:
Penny! That pinche zipper. Pennnny!!

PENNY:
I'm right behind you, Satan.

MEL:
Have you been keeping watch, my lil'
burglar detergent?

PENNY:
Hell yeah. Why you ask? What!

MEL:
I found a fish scale inside my alligator
suitcase. A fresh one.

PENNY:
It's like sand on a beach.

MEL:
The beach, yeah, okay.

PENNY:
And the sun heats up your cabana.

MEL:
The sun and the beach. I got it. SOB.

PENNY:
Alright then. Don't worry. Your
secret's safe with me. (winks)

EXIT MEL FUMING.

PENNY:
Between cleaning trout and clipping
eagles I've got a busy schedule. Shoot.
Where'd I leave my Louie Vuitton?

EXIT PENNY, SEARCHING. ENTER JEFF WITH PURSE.

JEFF:
What is this? It's heavy. It clanks.
Whoah, is it what I---

ENTER BOY.

BOY:
Thanks, Jeff. Appreciate it.

BOY GRABS PURSE AWAY FROM JEFF. HE PLAYS
KEEPAWAY
WITH IT.

JEFF:
Hey. I found it. It's mine. Come on, Boy.

BOY:
Well, I left it for two seconds. Now I
know who I can trust.

JEFF:
Sure. Honest Jeppo, that'sa mia.

BOY:
Here. Here's a Payday I found floating
beneath the pier. Knock yourself out.
You stuffed your own celery, peanut.

JEFF:
No kidding? Priceless. Great.

EXIT JEFF EATING CANDY.

BOY:
This bag of rands is a windfall for the
enterprising man awash in Doomsday's grasp.

BOY EMPTIES PURSE AND TOSSES IT ASIDE, THEN
FILLS HIS BANDALERO WITH COIN. POCKETS IT.
ENTER PENNY FRANTIC.

PENNY:
Anyone who helps me find my property will
be so well compensated. Sated. Have you
seen—

BOY:
I ain't seen jack, Fran. No bag, no swag,
no leather strap neither.

PENNY:
How do you know exactly what I'm—

BOY:
Psychic, darlin'. Go check your nooks,
your pits 'n' cans, your 'ills and valleys.
Hotcha.

PENNY:
Don't let Mel Miza catch your rat paw

red handed, Pancho Villa. Or your tortilla
flattery will be mud and battery!

BOY:
My fingers are so beige it's anti-climatic,
precious. Can I borrey--? Some dolor.

PENNY:
Oh no. Don't try to change the subject,
overlord. You raccoon. No kisses or cooties.

BOY:
That's eyeliner to keep the glare down.
You should try it. Come by later. I'll
fix you up, sis. And you do need vixen.

PENNY:
Are you punk enough to deep out of? Wilt
enough to stone my interest? Crash enough
to flame behavior? Drier than the cry of
sadness? Dark enough to shade my razor?

BOY BACKS UP AT THIS RECITAL. EXIT PENNY MAD.

BOY:
Ill-gotten gains, suspect goods, fill the
tool box until they spill. Gotta go stash
my Liberties. Oh happy day, where eagles fly.

EXIT BOY. ENTER MEL MIZA.

MEL:
Something's fishy with my luggage. Oh hell.
I gotta get the culprit. I'll place a

mouse trap inside the alligator. It's sure
to trap the devil abusing my sweeties.

EXIT MEL. ENTER MEATBALL WITH GEL HANGING
ON
HIS SHIRTTAIL.

MEATBALL:
Get away. Shoo. Go on.

GEL:
Why don't you bang and bruise me anymore?
You hardly choke and snorkle my selzer
waters. Moreover all my fruit is slick
and green as a new avocado. Bruiser!
What's wrong with me, huh?
MEATBALL:
I have goobers to pluck and hooplala to
inspire. Stars to unravel; worlds to
set afire. And my balls go...

GEL:
But--but--but---all my best I give to you.

MEATBALL:
Ah; boring. Done dat. Gotta move on,
sidewalk. Kick the can down the road.
Take the bucket--to Mr Beajingo.

GEL:
Oh. Okay. That's how it is. Well when
you're fifty fathoms down and need a
breath of fresh air, the kracken up yo
butt, don't look to me, driftwood.

EXIT GEL MAD AS A WET HEN.

MEATBALL:
First I'm radioactive. Then I'm the
bogey man. Sheesh. New horizons.
And my balls go jingle, jangle, jingo.

EXIT MEATBALL. ENTER KICKING ANTELOUPE.

KICK:
There's a sump pump in the ocean making
the fin swim round. Now I wish I were
an octopus, a crawling through the sound.
I see a school of hammerhead cruising
through the gulf, eating through cans
of tuna until they've had enough.

EXIT KICKING ANTELOUPE. ENTER MEL MIZA.

MEL:
Stab me, manta ray. Thread me a necklace,
man o'war. Tear my limbs asunder, great
white eyes. Reduce me to a krill. Grab
me, tsunami. Turn me into Miami sand.
Uh huh. Oh oh.

EXIT MEL MIZA WITH BEAR TRAP, WHICH HE OILS WITH WD-40. REENTER MEATBALL WITH CRACKERS AND CHEESE WHIZ.

MEATBALL:
What'll happen if all the real men folded
into nachos?

TWO ANGELS FALL FROM HEAVEN. MEATBALL EATS CRACKERS REGARDLESS, SITTING ON PILE OF NETS.

FIRST ANGEL:
Oh selah.

SECOND ANGEL:
Jumpin' Jehosaphat, that was a long way
to tumble. And it was all your fault,
Andreas. Trouble blankets your days.

FIRST ANGEL:
No, it's all on you. No conscience.
You started it. Drunk!

SECOND ANGEL:
You didn't have to follow and swallow,
blind bat. I was only using the diversion
so you could hightail it from the clouds.
Whassat?

FIRST ANGEL:
A pint of corruption. Taken from the stash
of the Pale Angel's saddlebags. Goood.

SECOND ANGEL:
What does corruption taste like? Is it
like bourbon, champagne, soda?

FIRST ANGEL:
On my sword, it's strong. Makes the frogs
woorble, lizard urk, the fish dribble, and
the turtles jerk. (shakes) There. Ah!

FIRST ANGEL TOSSES EMPTY VIAL AWAY. IT LANDS BY MEATBALL.

SECOND ANGEL:
What now? You drained the creek.
FIRST ANGEL:
I guess we sit back and watch these mortals gyrate and swim. Sputter and grasp. Chase conch, tickle eel, reduce their dogs to puddles.

SECOND ANGEL:
The morbid shuffle. That age old jag.
FIRST ANGEL:
It suits our shark skin hide. Down. Let's search for urns of Roman vino.

ANGELS ONE AND TWO DIVE BENEATH THE WAVES. MEATBALL HIDES TO WATCH AS TIM ENTERS WITH KRISSY, CAT, AND JEFF.

TIM:
I feel so hot. My periscope's foggy.

JEFF:
What do you know, hoot owl?

TIM:
So thirsty. This paddling dango is taxing. My only relief is dreaming of my angel.

KRISSY SPLASHES TIM. ALL START TO WET EACH OTHER IN SALT WATER.

KRISSY:
There you go. Cool down.

TIM:
Get off of me. Suddenly I can't see straight.
My eyes. Clouds descend and hover.

CAT:
He's in lust and too hot for one canoe.

JEFF:
Or he's zonked out by the gulf between
real and imagined love.

KRISSY:
Who's the latest sex symbol on our cruise?

CAT:
Pinche Penny. The tiger with a golden halo.

JEFF:
Penny that keeps on turning up like a
droll hooker. You don't love her.

TIM:
I would that that were so. Then I'd be
cured of this mortal blinders.

JEFF:
I have the answer for Cupid's folly.

TIM:
Great. Gimme.

JEFF SLAPS TIM.

JEFF:
And from now on you stay away from my
Pen-pen. She's with me. All mine.

JEFF KICKS TIM FOR GOOD MEASURE THEN HE EXITS.

TIM:
Bastard. Wait. My vision's clearing.
Hit me again, dealer! Send me, Sullivan.
KRISSY:
Goofus. Mad.

CAT:
Bonkers. Wet willy wigwam.

CHEVY ENTERS AND WALKS BY.

TIM:
Let me rest, harpies.

KRISSY AND CAT EXIT. MEATBALL MOVES FORWARD. HE KICKS ANGEL'S VIAL, PICKS IT UP. THEN HE POURS A DROP OF LIQUID
FROM VIAL INTO THE CLOSED EYES OF TIM. ENTER PENNY.

PENNY:
What has nine lives but only eats chow mien?

MEATBALL:
Are you the tigress that stripes my

zebra soul?

TIM:
Can't take a nap for the caterwauling
I swannee. Husha.

PENNY:
To its boo it will be true. Did you
abscond with my Louis, purse impounder?

MEATBALL:
Zipline, I'm mesmerized by your floating
isle and cold ears and expire tripping.

TIM:
Turn it down a little bit huh?

PENNY:
If you scratch it you won't kick it,
goal post. Even if you're a Pele
volcano.

MEATBALL:
I will so cherish your Saragossa seaweed
garden. Out of the seas, I scale creation.
I scale creation.

TIM:
If only Justice would quit rocking the
Libran scales. My calculust is taking
a powder.

PENNY:
If you play Verdi, wattle I get? A

pullet sore prize. Sing a lullaby
elsewhere, Casanova. After I pop two
notes and rock the heavens, it's time
to cool Venus's clam, mop Figaro from
the aria.

TIM:
Why can't the pearl diver save the
mother-of-pearl suds for a Christmas
toast over a fire of roasted pig?

MEATBALL:
It seems a cuckoo fantasy when I
try to commit foul murder, my hennaed
princess. Every morning I compose
Mein Cock! to apprise the warbling yawn.

PENNY:
This is one bizarre barnacle.

PENNY EXITS. MEATBALL FOLLOWING.

MEATBALL:
Wait! Wait! Surrender to the eddy,
release your salmon eyes to the riptide.

GEL FROM BEHIND A PILE OF BOARDS, DUCK WALKS
FORWARD. SITS ON HER HEELS.

GEL:
Silicon false silicone, why have you hexed
my beau? Now that I eat alone, can't fill
the catacombs. Each sad night I thrash on
foam, wandering dreams I do not own. Silicone

demon megaphone, men sway like metronomes. (dancing)
Wasted batch of titty foam, lily cyborg
microphones. Puberty-formed' chests remade,
fly catching marmalade. Moustache twirling
silly hommes, femme fatal zylaphones. You
see what mad science does inflating the cost
of love. Lazer locked on missle germ, pants
pressed and zipper firm. Zithers bow and
lyres twang, recognize the odes they sang.
History mark my plaintive song; once again
I run along. Popping bubbles and chewing gum,
singing songs and kissing bums. Oh silicone,
fast silicone, why have you wrecked my 'bode?

GEL RETREATS TO CRY.

TIM:
This mess of rope and nylon makes for
the worst hammock ever created for man
to wallow in. I'm ready to supplement
my lack of liquid with fresh red fish,
calamari, or even Bluefin. Tim, Tim,
you're my man. Add some vinegar, cuc,
and pickle my spam. Cucumber, Cucumber,
let me lead your jerkin's Braille as we
hail the supernova and gamma ray swale

.

TIM FASHIONS A THROW NET AND TOSSES IT. HE HAULS IN A CASE OF BOTTLED WATER. HE TOSSES THE NET AGAIN. EXIT GEL.

TIM:
Water! I'm safe. Tim, Tim, my Bim
Bam Bing, oh dawg, you pickle; you're

my best maid—

TIM PULLS UP A WOODEN PUPPET.

PAPI:
--snack oh Jack, you so zesty and so crispy, you frog my lily, my heavenly smack.

TIM:
Uh.

PAPI:
Good, quiet. Tim, oh Tim, every womin's friend. I hear the din of your late night train comin'. Come on. Lover, zow! Geni in a bottle, super nova star flow, mayo spam.

TIM:
Are you a robot? (shaking Papi)

PAPI:
Don't shake a screw loose, goose. I am your shadow. Stop shaking me. You'll muck up the batteries.

ENTER GABBY.

GABBY:
There you are. Hiding from the sun. Good for you. Water! Oh thank God.

GABBY GRABS CASE OF WATER. LEAVES.

TIM:
What is going on?

TIM TAKES PAPI THE PUPPET AND THROWS IT OVER HIS SHOULDER. JUMPS TO A DIFFERENT CANOE.

PAPI:
We jump and hump from sphere to sphere,
and even Alas! do some quantum jumping.

ENTER YACHT IN BACKGROUND PLAYING SALSA.

CAPPY:
Hey, sunfish and pikers. How's the
gravy in biscuit verde? You wanna
join us on a smooth cruise? La la
bomba rumble. We got fish sticks in the oven.
Plenty buns. A lit griddle.

TIM:
Yeah, if hookers were edible under
that ecstasy glaze.

BOY:
Howl now, clap later.

MEATBALL:
I wouldn't rent Fido's leg out to
that bum. Something's fishy and I
don't mean Catalina's choppy cove.

CAPPY:
You wanna a little snark, come over,
join us.

GABBY:
You go ahead with the skull tattooed
head stewardess. We'll call you if we're
bored. Drowning. Burning and itching
for crab.

PENNY:
If we were going down like Lucy there, uh..

LUCY:
Done caught a mess of lippy sirens no denying.

CAPPY:
Okay. Don't say I didn't offer. Ciao.

YACHT EXITS WITH PARTYGOERS. HONKING HIS HORN FOR THE RIGHT OF WAY. WAVING. GESTURING FOULLY.

TIM:
I was unloading some crap for the sleepy deeps,
Jetisoning fibrous ballast from my smelly keep,
When a rogue wave came along, slapped and dipped
the rear end of my sinking battleship. Whoah,
I cried to the snappy waters, don't you wash
away this sea horse and the fodder. Dancing
dolphin line waltzed with the shark to chase
my football across the salty pork. My deposit
was feeble reminder for the dim wits to never
give another sniff to my shift. My roe are

like caviar to enliven the trail of the dead
bodies. The bodies following the wake of that
dear yacht.

GABBY:
Yucko. You're sick, infirmo.

BOY:
Sad but true. See the red foam behind the yacht?

KICK:
I gotta sit down.

GEL:
What is it, Pops?

KICK:
The crows along the road all of a feather,
punctuate the high wire on a sheet of weather.
Here.
KICKING ANTELOUPE HOLDS OUT HIS TRIDENT,
THEN
MOTIONS TO THE SEA. GEL IS LEFT HOLDING
TRIDENT.

GEL:
What do I do? To keep it glowing.

GABBY:
Shake it.

KRISSY:
Stroke it.

CAT:
Rub and tickle it.

MEATBALL:
Think solar, act noble.

BOY:
Let me senile.

VARIOUS KIDS:
Check the lines. We need fish to live.
My fish ate my rod. My pole's gone too.
Who took my reelality? Hey that's my line?
You did it. Fess up! Weasel in the
shed!

KRISSY:
I can't fish with thieves. Cat burglars!

ENTER BLACK MAN ON LOG WITH FISHING LINE
TIED
TO A PLASTIC COKE BOTTLE. A KID SITS BEHIND HIM
BAILING WATER FROM
ONE SIDE OF LOG TO THE OTHER.

NAT:
There's a catfish at the end of the line.
I don't wanna bring her in 'cause it's snoozin' time.
There's a truck on the bottom fresh from a robbery.
You got the scuba gear you can go collect the keyes.
Gotta believe, gotta believe. Few wanna see God you
gotta believe. Wanna climb the Tree of Life not stuck in
an oak tree. To have a gander, you gotta believe.
Gotta believe, gotta believe. To commune with

the trees, you gotta believe. Well, boy?
SKIPPER:
I'm bailing as fast as could be. Moving the Pacific waters to the Atlantic. For balance and Justice.

NAT ON HIS LOG STREAMS ALONG. KID STILL BAILING.

GEL:
Calm down, creatures. Moco beasts.

TIM:
Easy for you to say. You got it all goin' on.

BOY:
Quit hittin' on my sister, moonpie.

GABBY:
But what are we gonna do besides argue?

KICKING ANTELOUPE MOTIONS WITH A CURVED FOREFINGER.

BOY:
Alright, mates. Who got that?

GEL:
Drop the anchor. Drop the hook, Tinker Bell.

THE YOUNGSTERS DROP THE ANCHOR DOWN, THEN PULL IT UP. THERE APPEAR LINES AND LOST RODS.

TIM:
I bet you're proud.

GEL:
Of course, we'd be lost without his demented hide. Untangle. Keep fishin', worms and minnows.

KRISSY:
Is your dad okay? He's shaking like a leaf.

GEL:
He's just dreaming of better days to come. After the ice age bites our butts. And the wooly mammoth returns its ivory. The miniature horses beat along the painted plains. When whale and cephalon rule the reefs and sandbars once more. When tribes dot the hills and hunger is a past memory. Yep. My dad dreams a fine life into being. His thoughts align with the Great Spirit's. Once the travails are over--he sketched out everything to me--the Spirit will send a sign, like the rainbow. But it's up to us to endure these trials of blood and fire, and to swirl the dark stripe of these shoals.

KRISSY:
I hope we make it.

MEATBALL:
The shoal must go on. Why is that star goin' backwards?

BOY:
Retrograde.

KICK:
Love.

GEL:
It's the planet of love and beauty. It rules the New Age.

TIM:
Hubba moma. Go on.

GABBY:
Ha. The evening star, the morning, star. The point to place a Titan rocket.

GEL:
It's the mystery planet clothed in fog. All we know about her are her togs. At times it's rumored, planets have taken a sabbatical, to visit the muggins.

TIM:
Right. When everybody's nackered.

BOY:
Oh you waif. If you want to impress someone, you grab their life jacket. Act!

BOY GRABS GABBY AND KISSES HER.

GABBY:
And what planet was that? Mars?

BOY:
Howdy doody, I'm sure. What? Have
the heavens thrashed your leather tongue?
Turn to suede it oil slick duck feathers?

JEFF:
Got one. Got a mullet or flying fish.

GABBY:
Oh boy, Boy.

BOY:
Less gab, Gabby, more grab I always say.

GABBY:
Hands down, sailor.

BOY:
Tell me you want to raise your sail.
There's a fire in the sky burning like
a pile of leaves. And there's stars
'round my eyes Whoah! like you won't believe.

GABBY:
Trust the heart in my torso and the fluid
in my veins for the horses run their corpus
in the heat and the rain.

JEFF PULLS IN A FISH.

BOY:
The moon is full with cows in the grass;
time to squeeze the utters and butter
Kaisars at last.

GABBY:
Oh sing to me of love before I sink into
the sod. Kiss my salty chin and wing
this bird to God; my valentino.

BOY:
I'll teach you about hawking, my lil dove,
but only if the bird stops chirping when push
comes to shove.

GABBY:
These kingfishers have got it covered.

BOY:
Let's hook up, my anxious lover.

MEATBALL:
And his balls go jingle, jangle, jingo.

GABBY AND BOY RETREAT TO A PILE OF BLANKETS.

ALL KIDS:
Dark Night, Dark Night of the Soul. Many
a squid will rock 'n' roll through the
Dark Night of the Soul.

A PIGEON LANDS ON MEATBALL'S HEAD.

MEATBALL:
Why me, Lord? My halo was never there. Now there's dookie in my hair. What does it mean?

GEL:
Lunch is served. The gods knock us down. Then they give us wings.

TIM:
Says the girl with Thousand Island underpants.

KICK:
Land.

ENTER SINGER AND SALLY IN KAYAKS.

GUIT:
We have no time to check Fate's teeth.

SALLY:
Get out your wrinkled skin; let's kick through the woods.

EXIT SINGER AND SALLY. BOY RETURNS TO STRUT.

BOY:
Here we go rowing through the fog.

MEATBALL:
Keep on slapping leather, Bucko. Wild ride that rules the world. Pigeon, get thee gone. Off.

FOG ROLLS IN. DRUMS SOUND.

GEL & BOY:
Pah tah hey. Pah tah hey. Pah tah hey.

KICK:
Eeh wah ho. Eeh wah ho. Eeh wah ho.

GABBY:
We must be over an Indian burial ground.

GERONIMO RISES FROM THE WATERS. HE CLIMBS ABOARD NEPTUNE'S RAFT.

GERONIMO:
When the new Ice Age arrives, Kicking Anteloupe, reclaim all the Indian Lands from ocean to ocean. For this duration, the grasses won't grow and the streams won't flow. So, treaty over. And our wait for the terms to expire, has come. Hey ya hey ya. Eeh wah ho. Eeh way ho.

KICK:
I hear you, Grandfather. Rest easy. We will recover our hunting and fishing and sacred burial grounds.

GEONIMO:
It is good. Hey ya hey. Nice pigeon hat.

GERONIMO SINKS BACK INTO THE WATERS.

MEATBALL:
Well, that beats the badger bone toss by
a yard and overshadows the Ghost Dance
ceremony by a cave bear claw. Neat.

TIM:
There's nothing wrong with a little heads-up
is there?

GEL:
Don't get your hopes up, goober.

CRAZY HORSE RISES FROM THE WATERS RIDING HIS MOUNT, WHO TRIES TO BITE EVERYBODY.

CRAZY HORSE:
Someone want to trade their tobacco for
this hellion? I got a terrible yen for
some leaf. Go, dog soldiers. Grab those
ponies and the squaw. Just leave me a
honey to smoke my buffalo. Ha yah hay.
Ha yah hey. The grizzlies are huffin' for me.

CRAZY HORSE SUBMERGES AS HIS PONY BITES A FLYING FISH IN TWO.

KRISSY & CAT & JEFF:
That was awesome.

BOY:
Now we're slappin' tuna.

TIM:
I love the sound of haunts, the goblin

serenade. Should we gather in a circle?

GEL:
As in, circle the canoe?. Seriously.

TIM:
Hold hands like a séance.
GEL:
These spirits don't need a knuckle knocker.
Someone dampen the aethers rather. Don't
try to filter these waters, humpback.
Accept it in the spirit that it's given in.
What time is it?

ALL KIDS:
Time to land a lunker. Boom shocka locka.
Whoah! Supper time.

TECUMSEH RISES FROM THE WAVES.

TECUMSEH:
These cedar choppers ain't just tradin'
for wampum, no sir. They are tradin'
fox tail for small pox. Meal for measles.
Bollocks for cholera. And there's no end
in sight to the white eyes. While there's
not enough coals to keep the fire goin'.
Nice earrings, Missy.

GABBY:
Uh, thanks? Mel Miza had them gathering dust.

TECUMSEH:
I'm gonna go on looking for pearls. So long.

TECUMSEH SPEARS OFF INTO THE WAVES WITH A POUCH BETWEEN HIS TEETH.

PENNY:
We've got a disturbance inside the Great Barrier Reef. I osmose it's a shawk that's come to shred my beef.

DENNY:
What gives? Why the warriors in the water?

GEL:
We're on the graveyard shift, sweetie. Get used to it.

CAT:
You'll never get bored once Doomsday drops her drawers.
DUST FALLS THROUGH THE FOG.

TIM:
Cover up your maws. It's Dusty Rhodes from here on out. Did someone invoke a Rhode Island red? Fess up, sinner. Time to eat crow.

REENTER SINGER AND SALLY.

GUIT:
Dusty was so lusty he wore out his tuxedo. Lucky for him though, underneath was a Speedo. Dusty was the kind of lad loved his bacon and eggs. When he chased hairy women he'd land on his head.

SALLY:
Dusty's gusty as a tornado in Oklahoma;
after six strikes he'd finally hit a homer.
He fanned the plate with his bat then
sniffed four balls like a hacked up tomato.

SINGER & SALLY:
Trust in Dusty, his spit ball was money.
Trusty lusty Dusty, dirty as a flea.

MEATBALL:
What are yawl doing stalking us, huh?

GUIT:
There's no place to park a kayak in
this ballpark.

GEL:
You're welcome to join our spread. The
party's just getting started.

GUIT:
Namaste.

SALLY:
Shalom.

KAYAK SETTLE NEARBY. MEATBALL MOVES ON
GABBY.

MEATBALL:
Oh golly, Holly Molly, tan me with
your body.

GABBY:
I'm afraid you'd be played by this
pork chop. By time dinner comes, you'd
be so hocked, pawnshop.

MEATBALL:
Ah yaggers! Every time I make a pass,
someone else scores with their pig skin.
I dispise fried port cracklings; I'm more
of a steak 'n' potato kind of guy. Spud
mignon at your Brussel sprouts, Mack Hollandaise.

GABBY:
No frog limb, amphibian. I am so sorry
that I have eyes, hands, a nose, psychic
tenacles. When voting for the body politic
that's just the way the campaign goes.

MEATBALL:
So I'll keep your advice filed under The
Bird.

GABBY:
I never took you for---

MEATBALL:
Literate. Smart thinking, sound bite.
I get that a lot. I'm the voice of
bison. I am the ghost of rolling thunder.
I am the voice--I am the flesh that trembles
when you wish. I am the figure that chalks
thee; glych that sigils Angel from Abyss.
I am the sigh, I am the sire that asp'rates
each and every one of us. That switches us

and hits us good. That craters each rock
of us. I am the Loan that must be redeemed.
I am the cost that crosses hush. I am the
sap congealed, I the vapor fief. I am
the passing blown zephyr seal. I am the crack
of the Mind that splinters the id kiwi
to sip up the sublime.

GABBY:
We only kill the ones we love.
Earth to angel, release the pigeon.

PIGEON FLIES AWAY.

BOY:
Moose whistle traffic stop wolf howl
accompaniment. Frog chorus gloaming
where Polly wogs mounds of meringue.

GABBY:
Thank you for the history lesson, Professor
Hedgehog. Don't pale from your shadow once
the sun blazes.

MEATBALL:
That's groundhog, Sarah. And thank you
for shrinking my coconut back to a
peanut.

PENNY:
So we have equilibrium. Before you know
it, the crabs and the mussels will be
pinching and squirting like a hoard of
Lilliputian firefighters slamming pickpockets

and borrachos at their picnic grounds.

GABBY:
Let me outta 'ere, nautilus. Phew!

MEL:
Tell it to the priest, sinner.

PENNY:
It's at times like these I wish I'd
been more discrete.

MEATBALL:
Than let's say, a hive-swarm of killer bees
kicked over by a piker.

THUNDEROUS HORN SOUNDS. THE PROW OF A
CRUISE
SHIP ENTERS FROM LEFT SIDE. A RED STRIPE RUNS
ALONG ITS WHITE
BELLY JUST OVER THE WATERLINE.
JEFF:
What a monster of the waves. Watch out
where you are poking your nose.

BULLHORN:
Ahoy, chippies.

CAT:
Wank!

BULLHORN:
This is the US Coast Guard on patrol.
All glory to the union and eminent domain.

CAT:
Quit hogging the planet, mutant lizard form.

BULLHORN:
We will be protecting the populace from any
manner of harm. Are you in need of assistance?

MEATBALL:
We have been incommunicado for days.

BULLHORN:
You heard the citizen. Do him proud.

AVOCADOS RAIN DOWN ON CANOES, RAFT, KAYAKS.

GEL:
Buckaroo!

BULLHORN:
You're more than welcome. Glad to be--
got a mayday. Bye.

GABBY:
We need water. Fresh water. Sun screen.

BULLHORN:
Indeedy it's a great day to be on the water.
Brown in the sun. Righteo!

BOY:
Another government pipsqueak mouthing
inanities like a Yellowstone geyser.
CRUISE SHIP CONTINUES TO PASS. EMPTY BEER CANS FALL. A SAILOR VENTS HIS BREAKFAST. THUNDEROUS

HORN BLASTS AGAIN.
GREENBACKS--MONEY--SHOWER THE WATERS LIKE CONFETTI. DUST FALLS AND INHABITS THE AIR.

CAT:
I could be in the Saharan desert. A
sheik on a camel canoe caravan shaking
in the storm of a sirocco blast.

BOY:
Ah, this dust. The talc is everywhere!
In my ears, my mouth, and my hair.

TIM:
It's clogging my nose, 'tween my toes,
in my food acting rude as the day, the
daze we don't have to see us through this
chalupa of pain and blood.

GEL:
I'm no cry baby but I wish I could escape
this awful earth aura. It's gotten
into my pores, my pants, my socks, my
shirt. Dirty dirty dirty snot.

KRISSY:
I can't get the scuzz outta my teeth,
my tongue, my tonsils. Now I'm getting
crow's feet.

JEFF:
Dust in Coffman, please go away.

BOY:
If you rinse your hole out with sea water
you end up just as foul and gritty.

GEL:
This dust prompts me to foal a tumbleweed.

GABBY:
Oh now, now, don't let a grimy surface
destroy your natural shine, wonderkin.
GEL:
Snap. Where's that singer to put this crap
into perspective?

KICK:
Ug.

KIDS:
We agree. This choking air, this dark cloud
of smog, this psychic shadow from the Beyond.

KIDS CLAP AND DANCE.

BOY:
This blanket of dust blocks the astral wind.

MEATBALL:
The muddy waters improve the fishing. I
caught a turtle. Now stew.

GABBY:
Oh yuck. And to think I listened to your
lines.

GEL:
You got some cleaning up to do, Meatball.

MEATBALL:
Dust clouds won't stop me. Darkness, please
be my friend. Water compounds us. Casting
my Garcia; the waters' eddy. Come on, gang.
Paddle on to Shangrila. So the wind smells
of sulfur? The devil waves his pee hole. But
I don't wonder because my mind is glassy.
The journey glides on forever for our fate is
to strive. Keep your heart tender and let
joy inside, let joy inside. Even if you pop
my hot cork, you'll find joy inside.

GABBY:
My God. You freak!

GABBY SLAPS MEATBALL, HIS HAND ON HER BLOUSE RIPS IT SOMEWHAT.

MEATBALL:
Got caught kneading my own cookie dough.

PENNY:
More discrete. Kept to female company,
passed on the tequila. But I was
flamboyant, hetro as the highways. Then
raged a thirst that shouted defiance.
Oh well. This's how life holds that
mirror to itself and leaves smeared
lipstick like snail tracked pathways.

PENNY PAINTS A HEART ON MEATBALL'S CHEEKS.

THEN SHE SMACKS HIS LIPS WITH MORE LIPSTICK ALREADY APPLIED TO HER.
ALL AT ONCE A BARGE RISES FROM BENEATH THE FLOATILLA OF CANOES, RAFTS AND KAYAKS. THE BARGE ENLARGES THEIR COMMUNAL SPACE.

KICK:
Life saver.

ALL KIDS:
You're not so mighty till you rise. You're not so flighty as surmised. Let's leave the might to fishing tales and hooking up with Jonah's whale.

CAT (to Meatball):
You know how to play checkers on a turtle shell? No! You ain't worth a donkey fart in Oaxaca.

MEATBALL:
Look, sweetheart.

CAT:
I'm a boy, jackass!

CAT TOSSES MEATBALL OVERBOARD, THEN SHE LEAVES IN A HUFF WITH TURTLE.

MEATBALL:
Oh hell. This dust is making a fine kettle of soup to be walkin' in. Pull me outta my rubber booties. Pull me outta the alligator shade. Crackin' crawdads by the fa'ar.

Cookin' marshmallows on my toenails.

GEL:
A golden hook, a can of worms, a box of shrimp,
fish till the morrow comes.

MEATBALL:
Don't condescend, mountain maiden.

GEL:
I'm not.

GEL HELPS MEATBALL BACK ONBOARD.

MEATBALL:
Right.

GEL:
I love a happy man. Full of vinegar. With
two left testicles.

MEATBALL:
Quit. Who's paying you to be nice?

GEL:
Leave my brother out of it. Uh...

MEATBALL (shrugs):
I need help fishing. Will you hold my
rod while I pee?

GEL:
The funny little man needs another bath.

I wish someone would slap some sense into
Mr. Potato Head! Hurry up.

MEATBALL:
I had a dream I caught my limit, unlimited
by bait or how long the fish played Go fish.
Poker then Slam me!

GEL:
Yes, all our days are rains and ashes,
pain and catfish, kicking down alleys;
to sweep a pathway. Mud filled pockets
and tightened sashes, pain and ashes,
pagan catfish.

MEATBALL:
I'm no pagan.

GEL:
Sure you are. Paying through the arts
for picturesque words, salting the tails
and pails of bristly girls. A trickster's
nose tickles them short. You're just
another snorting butter-me-not from a
Cowtown juke joint.

MEATBALL:
Hey I came to improve the stock of Camp
Wayward Kids. I've done my part. Paid
my way with pluck and dibs. Through these
canyons, now creeks of red. Through this
choke of berry flesh. Yelled at grizzlies.
Tweaked the wolf nose. Followed the compass
into the Unknown.

GEL:
(gag) You talk like a trailblazer in the
fur trade days at the Shasta's hemline.

MEATBALL:
Truth, injun? I'm lost and gray. But I
don't do this for myself. I do it for
the minnows, yeah.

GEL:
You'll make some gimp a fine jar of
cat food, Julio.

MEATBALL:
Girl, you're the darlin' of the wagon train,
the yoke that drives oxen insane. The
blanket atop the buttercups, lion cub and
lil' pup.

GEL:
You're the ozone when the lightning strikes,
the ghostly visitor creeping through the
night. The whirlpool whisking my egg whites
firm, the crazy hair on my tongue. The
lingering lingerie grinding bathroom burn.

MEATBALL:
You're the screen for my movie picture,
sound of laughter from a balcony of sisters.

GEL:
Got a sweet tooth. Let's see that kisser
Psyche! I'm not that easy, grease monkey.
Uh. Get off my hand. Gonna need it to wipe!

MEATBALL:
Ah, er, um, gosh. Lot of that goin' round.

GEL:
Go back to your Hustler stash, jeez.

MEATBALL:
In the alley. Third trash can on the left.
Where you left me, stalking. Ow. Who's got the
pliers to yank this golden hook from my palm?
Help, counselor? Yow!

GEL:
It ain't easy being cheesy; is it, Meatball?
Or you'd be name after Signor Parmesano.
Eh, pasano?

EXIT GEL.

MEATBALL:
I thought I was gonna land a whopper. Yelled
to the waves, Come to Poppa! But all I hooked
was my own hand. A psalm that bleeds within
the sandstorm's fan.

JEFF:
Shuttup! You're scaring the fish away. Chump.

MEATBALL:
My voice is hoarse as a stallion. Now I'll
rest in my galley.

MEATBALL PLUCKS FISHHOOK FROM HAND. FALLS ASLEEP--DREAMS OF STORMS AND ANGELS. GEL'S

SPIRIT FLOATS ABOVE MEATBALL.

GEL:
Cobra eyed emerald behind obsidian pleats of
kinky oblivion, Astarte spits the venom of love
across the feral mist; in lucent veins of
passion carved in soapstone union, her Isis
reveals arch hieroglyphs which sigis "occult
garden of the magic lotus where the thamaturge
lapis hocus pocus." Lunging with lofty hinge,
astral Horus runes his third eye Ka-like, twelve
gemmed nimbus of falcon frenzy on a throne of
feathered alabaster; ear omniscient crying...
cat goddess shimmer crowning the dolphin darkness.

GEL FADES

MEATBALL:
So what if the star's key is the fishhook?
You canna catch me, not the lightning.
Fraught in twain I slip 'n' slide.
Whisper innocence, angel confiding, open
up the glorious divide. Not you, though,
Glory. You think me a toad. And I confess
I'm ugly--long as woman peers through
Alice's glass. There to find a mushroom;
me! Nightsoil spawned. Fresh from the
Comet from Cigna 1456. Kids, away from me.
This is my hour.

TIM CRYING INTO A HANKY.

TIM:
Something's happening to my testicles. All

this wet has rotted them into peach pits.
Oh my God. Oh gosh. What's next? The short
stop to being a hermaphrodite? Should I be
brash? Yet I'm unabashed. And uncontrived for
being a proud morphodite?

REENTER KRISSY AND CAT, GIGGLING.

KRISSY & CAT:
Hey, Herm. How's it hangin'? Ha ha ha.
EXIT KRISSY AND CAT, STAGGERING.

TIM:
Oh hell, my scrotum's afire. My dinger itches.
(scratches)

REENTER GEL AND PENNY.

GEL & PENNY:
Ding, ding, ding, ring that bell. What is next?
Wishing well.

EXIT GEL AND PENNY.

TIM:
I've caught an STD, a fungus that turns men
into zombies. I'll try anything to get rid
of it, oh oh oh oh my, mommy. Yo yo yo I
got that zombie fungus; it spreads like
cunnilingus. It turns your scrotum purple
and inflames your dingus.

REENTER KRISSY AND CAT SINGING.

KRISSY & CAT:
Now you tool, do the zombie fungus. It only takes two to make a caucus; so join the circus and slime that octopus.

TIM:
Who has veneral lotion or anti-itch cream?

TIM EXITS RUNNING.

KRISSY & CAT:
Seaweed, seaweed salad. If I don't get some shrimp I'll go Madonna grabbing. Seaweed, seaweed—

EXIT TWO GIRLS. ENTER SALLY AND BOY.

SALLY:
This solar or lunar influence is loco. It turned a singer into a swinger. Now His pecker's fallen into the bait bucket. Good thing you're a virgin or else you'd have it too.

BOY:
Yeah, well. I'm not proud but—

SALLY:
It may spread in some arcane manner we don't recognize. Maybe we could try something different you know.

BOY:
What are you implying?

SALLY:
If normal hootchie kootchie is suspect for
you, well—

BOY:
I'd be remiss if I thought an ugly idea.

SALLY:
I'll turn around this way and clear the air.
Rub. Follow the bread crumbs.

SALLY BENDS OVER AND STRAIGHTENS UP. BOY FOLLOWS SALLY OUT. ENTER MEL MIZA AND LIL' BIT AND PREACHER LADY.

MEL:
What a bravo new novel is our novel. My motto
is "Bring on the dolls!"

LADY:
Oh Mel. Wonder Male. Mighty Mel. You the man.

MEL:
Little do they know I'm all plastic.

LIL' BIT:
How do you do it so long and firm while other
men turn back to worms?

MEL:
It's my genes. And my metal mentality.
Some men are muscular, but I am all brains.
During the night their locomotors fail. Not me!

LADY:
Oh wondrous. Profound. Seriously. Oh la la.
Yum.

MEL:
If there is an afterlife this must be heaven.
Oh my cherubim.
LIL BIT:
And thank you for these gold medallions.

LADY:
You are too kind.

MEL:
What!? I never--When did I squid and black out?

LIL BIT:
You left one of your bags open so—

LADY:
It's only natural. To share gelt with
your ringing belles.

MEL:
My bags. My randy rands. My band of buggers.

LADY:
That's what happens when you bare your
trombone, angel.

MEL:
If this keep happening I'll run out of
angels, er, barter items.

LIL BIT:
In another three years. Beyond the headstone,
because of the head and the boning, Mel,
you'll never be alone.

LADY:
Come on, daddy, come to Padre Island.
BOTH LIL BIT & LADY:
Bang your wang purse, the ladies sang. Up
and down the bunk bed. Man!
EXIT MEL WITH HIS GIRLFRIENDS. REENTER GEL,
TIM, WITH CAT AND KRISSY.

GEL:
Call me a kid again and I'll pull your
billy horn, loser.

TIM:
Maybe if you could scratch it a little. Huh?

KRISSY:
Show me that fast ball once again, Romeo.

TIM:
Now it's really just a curve.

CAT:
Is you or is you ain't: devil or saint?
Beat you to the deep end, squid face.
Inky. Inky.

TIM:
These are the times of storms and rip tide.
A storm is coming from space. Candles aflame.

MEATBALL TALKING IN HIS SLEEP.

MEATBALL:
I don't mind flying if it's a wet dream.
Otherwise lay me down in a pot of sand and
emeralds. Sure, sure, a spat of turbulence
to prove your over-weening manhood. Your
penchant for UFO dreams. Superman stories.
Fine, great, bring your kryptonite cloud
into my orbit and slosh me with radioactive
slime. How crazy jump the shrimp
trying to avoid being Moray eel hoe-down cakes.

THE ARCHANGEL GABRIEL ENTERS MEATBALL'S DREAM.

GABRIEL:
Come and close the golden circle.

MEATBALL:
Later, Gabe. I'll take a raincoat.
EXIT ARCHANGEL GABRIEL.

GEL:
Best wake up, whistler. You got a mother
of a bite on that line tied to your sole.

ENTER KICKING ANTELOUPE AND OTHERS. KICKING ANTELOUPE PULLS A ROPE TIED TO MEATBALL'S ANKLE.

KICK:
I know you been vampirizing my kitchen.
Search him. Find that doll.

BOY AND TIME GRAB MEATBALL'S TROUSERS. THEY FIND A VOODOO DOLL OF NEPTUNE COMPLETE WITH
NEEDLES AND BLOOD.

TIM:
Caught him red handed. Who has a hanky?

BOY:
You're in one Nosterafu snafu, jack.

MEATBALL:
But I didn't--it must have been the angel.

ALL KIDS:
Sure it was. Right!

MEATBALL:
The catfish woman in my dreams. My primo's trousers I put on in a rush to escape the sperm tossed husband. Cactus trans dimensional zombies!

KICK:
Nope. He's one them black mass priests with no dark gravity of his own. Tie him up with trout line. Bad mouthing the Pope before breakfast, ha!

CAT:
Get off the drugs before you drown Virginia. Sue Naomi's your woman.

KICK:
We'll use this chum for bait. Troll for a

giant hammerhead.

MEATBALL:
You guys got trans dimensional sickness no doubt. Tell me your moma's favorite ice cream flavor.

KICK:
It's uh--well, I can't recollect just now. That's a demonic question. Can anyone else recall that Blue Bell ice cream recall? See there? Wiped. The demon tongue wags.

MEATBALL:
Yep. Sure. You guys got it bad. Aah!

TIM:
No one's listening so scream till Doomsday comes.

MEATBALL:
Doomsday done hit, you blithering genius. Get that cow patty outta yer mouf. Hurble.

BOY STUFFS A RAG IN MEATBALL'S MOUTH.

BOY:
Talk your way around that one, silver tongue. Ah hell. These dark magicians are goofy. How the heck did we cop such a snitch?

GABBY:
Luck of the draw. All in the cards. Dead man's hand. An ace up the sleeve indubitably.

GEL:
And here he was trying to slip me a mullet:
the ole grouper. Don't act so snappy now do
ya, you lil scrapper. Urine the crapper!
His monofilament drew so fine it unreeled
a new paradigm.

KRISSY:
Snake! Snake in the water!

CAT:
Oh gosh, you sissy. It's not even two feet long.
I've had longer ones in my sand box to home.

KICK:
Got him tied? Well and good. Time to toss
the chump into the fjord.

BOY:
Bombs aweigh.

MEATBALL IS TOSSED BEHIND THE BARGE. BOY PLAYS OUT TROUT LINE. MEATBALL SPITS OUT RAG IN MOUTH.

MEATBALL:
Hey, where's my bobber?

BOY TOSSES MEATBALL A LIFE PRESERVER.

BOY:
There, you ungrateful corpse. With your
paisley eyes and spidery acne. That ball
of worms you call a hair style. Two

slug lips under a crawdad castle nose.

MEATBALL:
God bless you and the devil take you.
Glug-a-holler-and-splash-yo-moma. Work
her into your street corner playground
where the monkey bars never bar a gorilla
tortilla. Orange juice your cactus friends
as she squeezes Gomez for a banger covered
with musk gravy to salt her hairy donut.

BOY:
Don't make me—

MEATBALL:
Death's kiss, death's kiss, hold the tongue
and gift the bliss, bright red lipstick light my
wick. Onion breath, skoll head speaking
onion breath, fumes a-coming from your method
kill the flies spinning round my fez. Wishing well,
wishing well, seduce the senses and
calls upon the hounds of hell. Crazy love,
crazy love, just one more bug and wind gust you must
rise above.

BOY:
--come out there!

ALL KIDS:
I don't got a river to channel your cries
I don't got a boat to float your lies
I don't got an ocean to feed your wails
All I got's a bucket to help you bail.
(chorus:) All I got's a bucket to help you bail.

I know how hard it is to handle a canoe
I feel your tone singing the blues
I watch you ticking around the dock
All you gotta do is insert the notch.
(chorus) I can't supply the music for your dance
I haven't the gloss for wild romance
I've lost all feeling in my chest
Due to the drama of your TV set. (chorus)

TROUT LINE BURNS BOY'S HANDS AS IT FLIES OUT
OF
HIS GRASP.

BOY:
Daggummit. The best tied knots of
caps and mates, washed away by the tide
of fate. Ouch.

ENTER MEL MIZA.

MEL:
Someone has tripped my trap twice. It's
unnerving. But nothing seems to be missing.

REENTER TIM WITH A BEER AND PAPI IN HIS ARMS.

TIM:
I pulled up three cases of brew. We can
have a party for the crew. Look at my
dummy.

PAPI:
Easy for you to say. Wait till you're
floating in suds later.

A WHALE BREACHES THE SURF AND SWAMPS THE CREW.

GEL:
If I had a ladder I coulda kissed her barnacles.

TIM COMES FORWARD.

TIM:
These are uncharted waters. Hello everyone. Meet Papi, my alter ego.

KRISSY:
So cute. I didn't know you could throw your voice, Timmy.

PAPI:
Hey, girl. Let's get it on.

GABBY:
Wow. So studly. Does he have a--um...

PAPI SPORTS A RISING WAIST ROCKET.

PAPI:
I gotta woody just being close to you, cupcake. His name is Ole Hickory. Was once a cop's baton. Has a hard on for Goths and Weatherwomen.

GABBY:
Oh my. I want Papi to snuggle with later.

PAPI:
Oh cheri amor, precious as a breaching whale.

GEL:
My word, what a mouth you're flapping.

PAPI:
Please. It is not my mouth that's so imported. This joint comes from Italy and Brazil and France. I come all over the globe. All over you!

PENNY:
Don't you have all the moves, wildcat.

PAPI:
I do, Bride of Frankenstein. Plus all my moves can include you too. Just move your groove a lil' closer, I will take you over, a divining rod and a lover.

ALL THE GIRLS GIGGLING AND CROWDING AROUND.

PAPI:
Who's first? Let's get this party started.

ALL GIRLS CLAWING:
Me! Me! I saw the two-by-four first. I spoke up for lumberjacks. Scoot over and kick some other skateboard.

PAPI:
Ah so that's how it is. We will have to draw for the prize. For I can only do so

much. Time, she wastes us. Only one at
a time, for one wastrel. Now let's put
your button into my mouth, then we pick
eenie meenie miney moe. Just so.

BOY:
Dude, what are you doin'? Where we goin'?

TIM:
To hell in a trolley, to Hades for lunch,
to Valhalla for fajitas, the Styx for punch.

BOY:
You are a traitor to mankind.

JEFF:
You planted that voodoo doll so now we owe you?
Nut uh.

KRISSY:
What!! I can't believe my ears. I've got
tinitis of the ear, Tim. Someone answer the phone.

JEFF:
You are not blameless, you wet sock. Just
flameless as a rusty Bic.

KRISSY:
These mean tricks could come back to haunt us.
We're rocking on spooky shite caps, swabbie.

JEFF:
You got leagues to go before you can plant
your rag, critter. Girls! Girls! Order.

PENNY:
Two brats with relish.

GABBY:
Snitzel for my sourkraut, Forrest Gums.

CHEVY WANDERS FORWARD AND GRABS KRISSY'S ARM.

CHEVY:
Hey, I was wondering. Uh, um.

KRISSY:
Spit it out, bubble gum.

CHEVY:
Can I kiss you? Whenever you're ready.

CHEVY TURNS AWAY.

KRISSY:
People say it's puppy love. I don't care. He's my bud. I know I'm in love. And Prince Charmin he's my pup. Oh yeah. I kiss his nose fifty times a day. And oh, so often we go out and play. (chorus) Puppy love. Puppy love. Oh shut up, that's my bub.

ALL KIDS:
Puppy love. Puppy love. Oh shut up. That's my bub.

FLYING FISH JUMP INTO BOAT.

KICK:
Take cover. Watch your eyes.

GEL:
Oh boy. Free lunch. What could possibly
be bad about--Ow! Ow! Stoppit, shad!
Hide, hellions. Get under something.
Grab your darling, spin him round.

JEFF HUGGING GEL TO GROUND.

JEFF:
Heya, sugar. I gotcha covered.

BOY:
Workin' for supper. First the fish farm
mangles us, now we work it.

ALL KIDS:
Workit, workit. Grab that fillet outta
the bay, buoy. Workit.

CHEVY:
Let me fall into the mystery of your arms.

BOY:
Do whaa—

CAT:
Quit.

CHEVY:

Rescue dolphin with your mermaid song.
Blanket evergreens with chills of enlightenment.
Place an indelible kiss next your inscrutable
smile. Bounce the magic mirror of love on
my knees. Illuminate the shadows of your
seeking foal. Wash the mystery off your
gentle sphinx. And spell the Angel who
writes my soul.

CAT:
Talk to him. Go on.

KRISSY:
I can't. My face. Blushing. Stoppit.

CHEVY HAS FOUND THE BEER.

CHEVY:
Good mead, thick head, flight in a flask.
My nightly union, drink it with grass.
Great sack, sweet hay, nectar of Olympus.
Going down Hercules, coming up Vesuvius.
It is a blast. It makes ya trot. Gives
it a rise; then makes it flop. Mead,
guiness, porter, ale, lager. Dance like
a god; wake up a maggot. If you got no
one, it's your advisor. If you split your
ass, gravity makes your butt wiser.

TIM:
Why is that manta ray and the shark jumpin'?
What's scaring the monsters outta the drink?

GIANT TENACLE RISES OUT OF WATER. IT FEELS FOR FOOD ALONG THE DECK.

ALL KIDS:

The kracken!! We're dreaming. It's a nightmare!

CHEVY (drunk):

When I am dead and gone, it will be okay to slam me, call me a liar, make me the villain, style me a rogue, fool, and deceiver, rob me of my dignity and potato chips, shower me with purses and spiked flattery--bury me in dog dookey--but I ain't dead yet. I will be though. Soon enough.

OCTOPUS GRABS KRISSY AND PULLS HER OFF THE BARGE, RISING IN THE AIR. CHEVY PULLS ON TENACLE AND RELEASES KRISSY.
HE BEATS OCTOPUS WITH BROKEN BOTTLE. THE TENACLE TAKES CHEVY HOME INSTEAD.

CHEVY:

And I didn't even get to finish my first bock before I crossed the finish—

CHEVY IS PULLED DOWN INTO THE OCEAN. MANTA RAY FLIES ONTO DECK. IT STABS TIM IN THE THIGH. PAPI CRAWLS OFF.

TIM:

Ow! Damn it! Pull it out! Get that jasper outta me!

GABBY:

Said the dairy maid to the cow puncher

from a pile of straw.

GEL:
I got it, oh wanker.

GEL SLICES TAIL OFF MANTA RAY WITH A FILLET KNIFE. THEN SHE KICKS THE RAY OVERBOARD WITH JEFF'S HELP.

KRISSY:
Oh my God. Oh my God.

TIM:
Ouch! Omaha! Jota! Caramba!

GABBY:
You want I should operate? Get that
peckerwood out of your ass? Cut out
the barb?

TIM:
Yes, cut out the barbs and shiskabob
and get on with your barbarous job, Ratchet.

GEL:
What's wrong with this picture?

KRISSY:
Oh heavens full of gooses.

TIM:
Do it, you minx.

GABBY:
Are you promising me a mink coat for being your nurse? Awesome. No pressure.
GEL:
Who's barge is this anyway?

OTHER KIDS:
This is our barge. We trolled for it.

GABBY:
How lovely. I'm all mushy inside.

TIM:
Why am I surrounded by health care delinquents when I really need surgery?

KRISSY:
I'm gonna kill Vern when we meet at his book signing.

GEL:
We can't let some unwelcome creature come barging in on us. I demand privacy! Dignity! This tug ain't much admittedly, but it pulls me home, dig?

OTHER KIDS:
You shout it, siren!

PENNY:
I dunno. Somethin' you et. Cause your halitosis is atrocious. Ew!

GEL:
Every spare hand grab a knife, a toothpick
broken off your paddles, a smashed
mirror held by those mittens. And fight
back against this Jules Verne spermsack.
Come on, Vergil and Darrell, let's go!

KRISSY BITES TENACLE OF OCTOPUS.

PENNY:
I'll choke him if he don't breathe right.
But I hope he don't pass out. 'Cause
I ain't going down Junk Street. Seriously.

TIM:
What!? A blow job. Great, the perfect
anesthetic. My Nightingale in Goretex!
Sing for me.

GEL:
A fork. A fish hook. Break a broom and
stab! Give the bully a taste of its own
medicine. Boots, nails, elbows, teeth!

PENNY:
Hey, you don't pay I don't play, pitcher.
Now if you kidnapped me let's say, took me
to your lair. I caught Stockyard Syndrome
due to no straw, saltlick. Boredom. That be
different. Then I'd attack, like this!

PENNY BITES TIM'S ASS.

TIM:
Aaah!! Hellfire, Elvira.

GABBY:
Thanks, sweetie. Looks like my used tampon.
PENNY:
It was nuttin'. Like cuttin' a steer in
the Spring. Ha. Call me anytime you want
a diversion. Pinche Penny at your cervix.

MEANWHILE THE OTHER KIDS HAVE PUT THE HURT TO THE OCTOPUS AND THE CREATURE HAS TO WITHDRAWN.

TIM:
Keep that tramp shut, hussy. I can't hear
myself think. Oh no, I lost Papi.

PENNY:
I feed one hound, the whole pound's
ballooning afterward.

BOY:
Arrrhloo!

PENNY:
Scream your pimpled throat raw, purse
snatcher, while I give this poor boy
a post surgical massage to get his blood
back to flowing correctly.

TIM:
Oh. Oh. What! Wham! Whoah! Who?--Aah.

PENNY:
Yucko, Bucko. You keep the souvenir,
little doggie. A seven seas salute
offers up a seasoned solution, seaman.

CHEVY IS TOSSED OUT OF THE SEA AND BACK ONTO THE DECK OF THE BARGE. KRISSY STRADDLES CHEVY AND BEATS ON HIS CHEST.

KRISSY:
Don't break my heart, you dummy, don't
break my heart.

CHEVY REVIVES, VOMITS ALL OVER KRISSY.

CAT:
That vomit taste so good, hah!

KRISSY GETS UP AND KICKS CHEVY.

CHEVY:
What was that about?

KRISSY:
That's to cap your baptism. In salt water.
And mine in the soup of upchuck.

CAT:
At times like these, I like to think on
skate boarding and bicycle tricks. Chuggin'
sodas and spritzers beneath the bat cave
bridge. Pumping my fist at semi's jackknifed
and wrong headed. Black Panther
marchers catching rubber bullets after

saving chickens from 7-11 fires. Helping
little ole ladies tackle emus at Easter
lily gardens. Have a drink, Chevy. You're
gonna need ballast.

KRISSY:
I love the coolness of cathedrals on
Monday. Shaking hands with muggers before
I drop my screwdriver from their hip hipster
that don't run for months so sorry did that
behave next time, Peg Leg. Tossing golf balls
onto interstates in 5 o'clock traffic. Climbing
trees to avoid Jack the Rabbit night in the park.

CAT:
Freedom, that's democracy.

KRISSY:
Instead of one or two decrepit puds deciding
the Presidency in back rooms over Havanas and
Crown and coconut bookends.

CAT:
We the people who survived amendment.

KRISSY:
Amen!

ALL KIDS:
Amen!

KRISSY:
Claim as our domicile—

CAT:
Whatever hoodie still floats—

KRISSY:
Along Kracken Acres beside Boot Hill.
CAT:
We abolish ageism and nuclear—

KRISSY:
And why nuclear? I'm not clear why—

CAT:
Don't eat the glow fish. If isn't a
glow worm in the dark of your tent,
that be the guy from the next shack over
sleepwalking his dachshund for a midnight snack.
KRISSY:
How can you tell in the dark?

CAT:
I know you're a girl because you smell
of sunfish and moonbeams. Wait. I just
called myself a Mary.

KRISSY:
We left Suchi in Sacramento with Tahini
and Gumbo.

ALL KIDS:
All we got are pain and ashes, pain and
ashes, oh my captain. All our love for
bashing Ashley in the trash can, in the
alley. Save the pain for the Jacuzzi
stripping and the ash for rose bud clippings.

KRISSY:
After we eat Mary-nated fish I'm taking
a nap.

CAT:
Well, after that whale snack slap I'm
never gonna sleep again. That was the
whale that butchers rest, peace of mind
lost from the head. No more heaven floating
on my frame because Doomsday is quite insane.
Blow the horn at Gabriel's prompt but keep
away the ghouls and haunts. I want to
keep alive my pet frog and longing for
chicken but evermore the riptide gets thicker.
If I hear Taps I'll shake my noggin', pinch
my wrist, go off jogging. If you see me
bowled over, shake me wake: I'm sure I done
caught a water snake. Don't call for Cat.
I'm Snooze Walker.

JEFF:
Basket case.

GABBY:
I'll be so glad when our cruise comes
to an end.

BOY:
Watch out what you wish for.

GEL:
If I never eat another fish dinner, I'll
die happy as a pig swimmin' in a cranberry bog.

JEFF:
I wonder, are you the lioness that impales
my impala, Joesy?

GEL:
Go catch a bobcat, take her for a stroll.

BOY:
Oh no, I accidentally ate a krill.

GABBY:
That's a good thing for Neptune's child,
right?

KICK:
No telling. Where's Meatball? So quiet.

KRISSY:
He went off to collect crab and oyster—

KRISSY JABS JEFF.

JEFF:
For fish cakes, correct.

CAT:
There's a signal on the horizon.

KRISSY:
There's a horn blast through the swells.

CAT:
Fathers dance and mothers scamper.

KRISSY:
Get granny to run buy her pills.

CAT:
We'll choke on the air and wade through grit.

KRISSY:
Start a fashion for stashing our booze and our kill.

CAT:
Forget about a mud face and a rash of zits.

KRISSY:
Cry out for help to Uncle Sam calling it quits.

CAT:
You can't rely on neighbors or the convenience sto'.

KRISSY:
Steer away from robbers who only ask for more.

CAT:
Fly like a mosquito, and zoom, dragonfly.

KRISSY:
Get used to eating dirt like a pig in a sty.

CAT:
Billy harness the horses to win the next derby.

KRISSY:
If you want a loaf of bread best get up early.
CAT:
Who knew dollars be worthless as good ole TP?

KRISSY:
Go on pitch a tent and sleep 'neath a tree.

CAT:
Liberty is broken. Free speech passe'.

KRISSY:
If you want freedom then you must play, homes.

CAT:
Play the xylophone. Play the trombone.
Read the cards or toss the badger bones.

KRISSY:
Anything's better than TB or no phone.

TIM:
Take me away from normal eyesight.

GEL:
You got all that and more.

KICK:
I feel a quickening of the senses.

GEL:

Oh yeah. My spider's tingling in my
fly also.

KICK:
I mean my time is coming to bid yawl adieu.
GABBY:
If you abandon our Titanic, boy we screwed.

KICK:
Adios. Arriva dergi. Ciao. So long
Aloha. Tootaloo.

GABBY:
Five ticks in my stockings keep me itchin'
anyhoo. Well, it's been fun, Jason.

GEL:
Stoppit. Dad, you're just wiped. Rest
your eyes and I'll watch. Time takes
coke bottles, squeezes sand through its duo diem.

KICK:
No, I've seen the future and it's Luna City.

BOY:
If it's related to the spaghetti I just
wolved down, you ain't missed nuthin'.

TIM:
Speaking of witch, here comes the meat wagon.

IN DISTANCE ANOTHER RIGHT WHALE BREACHES.

CAT:
That's an awful lotta food truck lining up for luncha.

KICK:
Don't get any closer, Demon Blue. I will tear you leaf from limb, you bleached out Levi fan. I am the God of the Ocean. The King of the Waves. Do not challenge this aqua farmer or you'll mortgage Spain.

ALL KIDS:
All we are is pain and ashes, on the dole between two fascists.

GEL (dancing):
There's a message in the ethers and it isn't hard to find if you take the blinds off and wing your eagle mind. There's distinction in the cauldron; there's brouhaha in the stew. Simply open up your forehead and soak up Xanadu. We must test the Wheel of Fortune, it's the least that we can do. Burn the dross inside the mountain; all that's left we call it Truth. Take the boat across the river. Follow the shepherd to the hills. Do not worry about the narrows; face your fears and breathe your fill. There's a pennant we must follow, across the leagues to show we're game. Let's wrap Glory in a laurel; praise our Heroine and shout her name. There's destruction in the kingdom; there's a beehive on the coals. Witches

fly and broom stick blister. Find a cave
for the tribe to claim. A tool for dark
forces, a plaything for the gods. We tried
to ride the horses, but what did we do wrong?
One day predicated by the morrow; each step
determined by a heel of bread. Each stave
eaten by the oxen; each staff beaten down
by the row.

KICK:
Thar she blows!

KICKING ANTELOUPE CHALLENGING WHALE.

KICK:
Gimme my trident, guppy.

JEFF TOSSES TRIDENT TO NEPTUNE; THE WATER
GOD
PUSHES OFF THE SIDE OF THE BARGE.

ALL KIDS:
Oh!

GEL:
What! Whatta!

WHALE SWALLOWS NEPTUNE AFTER GEL TRIES TO
GRAB TRIDENT.

BOY:
Oh hell, that didn't happen.

WHALE DIVES.

ALL KIDS:
All our flames have fumed to flashes; past
the pain and kissing Ashley. You've let
your light shine into the shadows; your
love has exploded into the spheres. Now
that your mission has been accomplished,
blast through the final layer, my dear.
All our flashes reduced to amber; all
our urgency swept away. Send your spirit
off with the sparrows and let your arrows
win the day. All the flames have subsumed
into burbles, past the pain and tickling
girdles.

GEL:
Come back to me when you are through slaying
dragons and rocking the moon. Come back to me
when you've seen the world, spanned the
equator and straightened your curls. Come
back to me when there's nothing left between
the fight for thrills and the search for wealth
Come back to me when travel is ego death and
you want to hang up your brass for happiness.

MEATBALL BOBS ALONG IN WAKE OF WHALE.

MEATBALL:
Guys. Guys. Hep. That--whale--was--
allr-gic--to macho nachos dela mole.
I've been hollering after--you all--
day. Don't forget to right your Esse,
pop quiz. EEEEhhh!

GABBY:
Ug. Do we know you, pond scuzz?

ALL KIDS:
All our meatballs rolled to hash browns.
On the grill with potato mashers.
BOY:
Bottom feeders rise to the top of the
food chain. Kneel, Knights and Ladies,
of the Golden Section. Now rise, rats
and lemmings of the dawn of Doomsday, dummies.

GEL:
Who died and made you cardinal?

GREAT WHALE RISES. NEPTUNE'S HEAD IS AT THE
BLOW HOLE. KICKING ANTELOUPE PUSHES ARM OUT
THE ORIFICE. THEN
THE GUY IS BLOWN OUT OF THE BLOW HOLE, AND
UP-
-UP--UP INTO THE STRATOSPHERE. HE IS LAUNCHED
INTO HIS OWN ORBIT.
WHILE THE MOON IS ALREADY OUT, THIS NEW
SATELLITE JOINS LUNA AS AN EXTRA MOON. THE
GREAT WHALE DIVES DOWN.

MEATBALL:
Wow, there goes the waterdog of Judgment Day.
Now all we needs is the light of the sun. I
was in the great beast's belly twelve hours.
It was not too wet yet somewhat warm and
yes, steamy. I dozed. Learned to chew on
the small fry left over from grazing. My
advice? Stock up nuts and grains for

Armageddon Days.

BOY:
You lucky we forgot whatever it was we was thinking.

MEATBALL:
Sure. Now who could replace me?

REENTER PAPI ON PENNY'S LAP.

PAPI:
You're invisible. Harder to get rid of than a bear trap.

MEL MIZA COMES FORWARD.

MEL:
Do what?

PENNY:
Uncover, you spy.

PAPI TAKES BLANKET OFF HIS LOWER BODY. THERE'S A BEAR TRAP ON HIS LEG.

PAPI:
I was only looking for some furniture polish to restain my talleywhacker.

MEATBALL AND BOY AND TIM REMOVE THE TRAP.

PAPI:
I'm getting outta the fur trade.

PENNY:
And I'm gonna be a nun.

PAPI:
Switching over to sea lion and penguin.
ALL GIRLS:
Ark! Ark! Ark! Ark! Smooka locka.
Smooka locka. (cough, cough)
MEATBALL:
I guess that does it for our ark.

GEL:
Satellites fall with the meteors,
and new junk rises to take their
place. What? I can't hear that
apology cause you're stuck inside
Davy Jones' locket.

MEATBALL:
Hey, look. There's my whale taxi.
Toss the girl a fish, be responsible.
I am cupid's primo so never say
never, Chula. I will spice your
thighs. Come and grind this Pancho.
The hero in El Barrio, the spinner
at the laundry, a magician of the night,
full of cagy conjuring. With a high
forehead, a devil of a cleft chin,
climbing up Ivy's window to tune my
mandolin. The mirror of pachuco
loafers, the maestro anaconda, tossin'
Pegasus's horse shoe, diving after hot
nachos. I bend cupid's bow, come roast
my chili pepper. I'll stir the pot till

you pop, chrome you like a fender. Give
you'all a tup of svine, brook no argument.
All I'm proposing is squid pro quo, let
me be your samurai fish target.

GEL:
And that's all you got?

MEATBALL:
Well my balls go jingle, jangle, jingo.

GEL:
I'm appalled by your bragging, little
tango bingo.

CHEVY:
Yep. Vamos a Corpus Christi. (recites song)
Follow a vision mystical. Come gaze into my
crystal ball. Vamos to Corpus, you'all.

FINIS

www.ingramcontent.com/pod-product-compliance
Lightning Source LLC
LaVergne TN
LVHW040141080526
838202LV00042B/2980
* 9 7 8 1 9 5 6 0 7 4 4 2 0 *